CABIN LESSONS

CABIN
LESSONS

···· *A Nail-by-Nail Tale* ····

Building Our Dream Cottage from
2x4s, Blisters, and Love

SPIKE CARLSEN

Storey Publishing

*The mission of Storey Publishing is to serve our customers by
publishing practical information that encourages
personal independence in harmony with the environment.*

Edited by Carleen Madigan
Art direction and design by Jeff Stiefel

Cover photography by Jeff Stiefel (front), Jeff Johnson (cabin photos front and back),
and © Tom Thulen (author)
Interior photography by Jeff Johnson, except pages 11, 21, 34, 41, 52, 64, 76, 81, 96, 131,
168, 193, and 199 courtesy of the author
Illustrations by © Michael Gellatly

Storey Publishing
210 MASS MoCA Way
North Adams, MA 01247
www.storey.com

Printed in the United States by Versa Press
10 9 8 7 6 5 4 3 2 1

LIBRARY OF CONGRESS CATALOGING-IN-PUBLICATION DATA

Carlsen, Spike, 1952–
  Cabin lessons: A Nail-byNail Tale: Building Our Dream Cottage from 2x4s, Blisters, and Love
/ by Spike Carlsen.
    pages cm
  ISBN 978-1-61212-567-1 (paperback : alkaline paper)
  ISBN 978-1-61212-568-8 (ebook) 1. Carlsen, Spike, 1952-2. Carlsen, Spike, 1952—Family. 3.
Carlsen, Spike, 1952—Philosophy. 4. Log cabins—Superior, Lake, Region—Design and construction.
5. Vacation homes—Superior, Lake, Region—Design and construction. 6. House construction—
Philosophy. 7. Carpenters—Superior, Lake, Region—Biography. 8. Stepfamilies—Superior, Lake,
Region—Biography. 9. Superior, Lake, Region—Biography. I. Title.
TH4840.C37 2015
690'.8092—dc23
                          2014043111

To Dick and Jean Thorngren, who sold us the land, then gave us much more — full hearts, full stomachs, and full belly laughter. You will always be a part of Oma Tupa, Oma Lupa. Ain't that somethin'.

And to our kids — Tessa, Kellie, Zach, Maggie, and Sarah — who helped us build not just the cabin but also the family we are today.

CONTENTS

INTRODUCTION

Oma tupa, oma lupa.
(One's cabin, one's freedom.)
— *Finnish proverb*

In some families red hair and freckles are inherited; in others it's the talent to play baseball well or a predisposition toward skin cancer. In my family the urge to own a cabin runs deep in the DNA.

My grandparents had a cabin built for them near Brainerd, Minnesota, in the 1940s. They nicknamed it "The Roost" — and in doing so sentenced themselves to a never-ending torrent of birthday presents and thank-you gifts plastered with images of roosters. Their dinnerware had roosters on it. There were cock clocks, rooster-shaped spoon rests, and pictures of roosters combing their combs. The doormat had two roosters holding a welcome sign. My grandmother's embroidered apron sported a rooster running with a platter of food; on the platter was what looked like a roasted turkey, but that may have been rooster, too. Chickens, turkeys, or other barnyard fowl were not an acceptable part of the decor. It was strictly roosters.

Thirty years later my parents bought a small, run-down cabin on Lake Waverly, a one-hour drive from Minneapolis. My father wanted the cabin to be a family affair, so he set a rule: for every five hours a person worked, he or she would earn one number to the combination padlock that guarded the door. Fifteen hours of painting, raking milfoil weed, or untangling fifty years' worth of fishing line in the boathouse earned you cabin rights. He bought the cabin, proclaimed the padlock rule, bolted two old theater seats on the end of the dock for contemplating life, and then died with a tennis racket in his hand a few months later.

There were two morals to the story. The first moral: name your cabin carefully. When Kat and I built our cabin, we took the rooster

My sister, Merilee, and me at The Roost,
trying on Grandpa's fishing waders and boots

lesson to heart and named it Oma Tupa, Oma Lupa. Translated from its Finnish roots, it means "One's cabin, one's freedom." Unlike for roosters, there is very little *oma tupa, oma lupa* memorabilia available in gift shops. The second moral: we learned that life is short, so live and love while you can.

Many books are simply good, long allegories. In *Secrets of a Very Good Marriage: Lessons from the Sea,* Sherry Cohen uses fishing experiences as a way of examining her relationship with her husband. She offers such parables as "See the beauty in what he loves, even if it looks, for a minute, like ground-up fish bait." And "Spend time together: hearing about catching the shark isn't the same as feeling the shark's breath." A 1960s book called *Centering* by Mary Caroline Richards was, at face value, a book on throwing clay on a potter's wheel, but just below the glaze was a treatise on centering the soul as well. In *The Old*

Man and the Sea, Hemingway is wrestling with something larger than the marlin on the end of his line.

Likewise, we found building our cabin was more than just whacking 2×4s together. Designing a 600-square-foot cabin — a dwelling the size of a double garage — forced us to consider which things and activities were most important. Watching Kat, my wife, and Sarah, our oldest daughter, install deck boards at what to me as a seasoned carpenter seemed a glacial pace held a lesson in determining which was more important — a quickly built deck or the pride they felt in their newly honed skills. A thousand questions arose. Should we have blue or brown siding? Internet? Sleeping places for all five kids? A washing machine? Sex after insulating? A big or small kitchen sink? These were all questions we grappled with. Our cabin is the art of compromise memorialized in wood.

When some couples reach midlife, he buys a red Miata sports coupe and she gets a facelift and a walnut-size cocktail ring. Not us. We decided to buy a nearly inaccessible cliff of eroding clay on Lake Superior and build a cabin together — along with five kids, a handful of friends, and a half-blind, gimpy Pekingese. We decided from the start that the process of building would be just as important as the final cabin. And in the end we wound up with a cabin perched above three quadrillion gallons of water and a bucket of memories. Welcome inside.

I

WANTED
DIFFICULT PIECE
OF LAND

If you can't find a perfect piece of land, buy an imperfect piece and make it perfect.

MOST COUPLES WHO ENJOY each other's company nurture a relationship with a place as well as with each other. This place can be near or far; sophisticated or simple; metropolitan or rural. This extramarital affair can begin early or late in life. It can be a place of adventure or tranquility. There are few qualifications. It must be a place you consider "your own" even though hundreds of others may claim the same. The thought of going there must make your heart rate increase by twenty-five beats per minute. Blindfolded, you'd know you were there simply by the smell and sound. Cozumel, the resort sixty miles up the road, Central Park, a log on the banks of the St. Croix River — any place is fair game.

———

For Kat and me this place is the North Shore of Lake Superior. We stole away to dumpy little resorts along its fringes when we first met, kayaked across it on our honeymoon, were freeze-dried by it as we skied with our kids, screamed together as we locked arms with friends and plunged into its 40-degree waters, used its waves to soothe us when life was smothering us. So slowly, inevitably, the urge to buy land crept into our bones.

But this cabin idea keeps its distance — a feedbag hung before two stubborn mules that keep plodding forward. When we visit our first realtor and explain, with bourgeois bravado, we could spend, "Ohh, up to fifty grand," he gives us that "You gotta be kidding me" lift of the brow. We soon learn the economics of the dream are forbidding. We inquire about one cabin, only to find eight parties engaged in a bidding war. The ailing resort we frequented and fantasized about buying goes on sale for seven figures.

We light out on our own. We run **LAKESHORE LOT WANTED** ads in local papers. We get calls about land with **LAKESHORE VIEWS**, meaning land across the road, up a hill where you can catch a glimpse of the lake if the wind blows just right. We add the qualifier **DIFFICULT PIECES CONSIDERED** when we discover lots of the sort we ache for often fetch hundreds of thousands, not tens of thousands, of dollars. We view "nature areas" (mosquito-infested swamps), "cabins with potential" (mobile homes with rotted floors), and "rugged lakeshore" (jagged rock you couldn't stand on, let alone build on).

On our jaunts north we often stop at small-town realty offices hoping to hear, "Yumping Yehosaphat, I yust got a call from old Martha Wilkins down the shore, and she's been thinking of . . . " Never happens. One realtor diplomatically tells us, "All the snoots from the cities are driving land prices so high locals can't afford it anymore." We are those snoots, thank you very much. So our longing for land and cabin remains just that.

We continue to keep a **SUPERIOR LAND** folder stuffed with ads, brochures, and leads. In the back sits a photocopied piece of paper we'd pulled from a **TAKE ONE** box mounted beneath a realty sign. The day we grabbed this piece of paper was iceberg cold. The kids were weary from skiing and impatient to defrost. We saw the **LAND FOR SALE** sign, made a U-turn, and stepped out of the van despite the dreaded quintuple kid-moan. When we looked out to view the land, it was so steep we saw mostly treetops and lake. The survey on the back showed two pieces of land: one was square and normal-looking, the other shaped like a rhombus with a dunce hat. "Difficult land" is one thing, "impossible land" quite another. The paper languishes in the folder alongside our dreams.

———————

When you buy a lot or piece of land in the cities or suburbs, you buy more than a piece of land. You buy all the city council meetings it took for the developer to get the land rezoned. You buy the time of the lawyer who made sure the land had clear title and the time of the surveyor who plotted and marked the coordinates of each lot to the inch. You buy the excavator's time to rough shape the land, bury storm sewers to accommodate the fifty-year rainfall, and put in properly compacted asphalt roads. You buy a drivable driveway and an accessible building site. You buy a street and a sidewalk. You buy a city water line buried 8 feet deep so it will never freeze and the guarantee of pure, plentiful water. You buy a sewer connection that guarantees every flush and spittle of toothpaste will be ushered quietly and odorlessly away. You buy your electric service, natural gas, and cable, which are only a phone call and signed check away. In short, you buy certainty. You may pay $200,000 dollars for a barren 100 × 200-foot plot of ex-cornfield in Oak Haven — a lot that's a Rorschach image of the lot to either side — but that lot is Lloyd's of London, 100 percent guaranteed buildable.

When you buy a piece of virgin land along the North Shore of Superior, you buy less than a piece of land. You buy the uncertainty of land that's raw and wild — land where neither man nor nature has given forethought to a driveway, septic system, or water well. The land could care less if there isn't a flat spot larger than a school bus anywhere on it. It's neither snobbish nor well polished because it's perched along the shores of one of the largest, most powerful lakes in the world.

It doesn't fight back when 20-foot waves erode its banks. And there's surely no certainty that a dwelling — at least an affordable one — can be built there. You step up to the craps table, and while you may be well versed in the odds of the game, you can still get a bad roll. Mother Nature is the casino with the odds stacked in her favor.

On one land exploration jaunt we ask a North Shore Realtor to search the Internet for lakeshore lots based on price — we've finally upped our budget. Three options pop up, all bad. He scratches his head, pulls out a piece of paper bearing a piece of land in the shape of a pregnant stork, and in a single breath says, "This is at least close to your price range, and the owner makes great fish cakes." We have no notion of what a fish cake is and a strong feeling that the land he is referring to is the one suited for mountain goats we'd seen previously on a cold winter day. Yet we nod. He picks up the phone and hoots, "Hey, Dick, you old herring choker, there's a young couple that wants to look at your land." And I ponder, "At what age does one cease being called *young*?"

We drive down a steep driveway and find Dick Thorngren, the old herring choker, and his wife, Jean, standing on the porch. I step out of our truck demanding the promised fish cakes, visions of the *Saturday Night Live* Bass-o-Matic dancing in my head. Dick fires back, "Oh, you don't want to eat those before you hike the land. The grease in 'em will kill you." Jean shakes her head.

We introduce ourselves all around; then Dick loads Kat and me into a war-ravaged four-wheel-drive Ford F150 and heads down what could only generously be called a path. We cut cross-eyed across a steep incline, smash through overhanging branches, and bounce our way down toward the shoreline. I'm not studying the land; I'm too busy studying how we'll escape from a flaming, barrel-rolling F150 before it lands wheels-up in Superior. Dick stops short of a spot that holds the remnants of a boat launch he carved out of the shoreline thirty-five years ago when he'd dabbled in commercial fishing.

From there we look up and see the two pieces of land for sale. The one we're standing on has its allure. The parcel is three and a quarter acres. The 515 feet of shoreline is boulder-strewn, almost sculptural. The rise from shoreline to building site is solid, mature rock. There are pines, birch, and poplar aplenty. But it has its drawbacks. As fantastic as the shoreline is, it isn't easily accessible. There's only one logical building site — and that's close to the highway and distant from the lake. And the price tag makes us weak in the knees.

We walk toward a point jutting 60 feet out into the lake. A survey stake with a blue flag divides the point in half.

"I couldn't make up my mind which parcel should get the point, so I split it right up the middle," Dick later explains.

We walk to the end and turn around. The boundary line between the two lots, marked by blue ribbons, zigs to accommodate a future driveway and zags to accommodate splitting the point. Its legal description requires eighteen lines of bifocal-straining print.

Above us to the right perches three acres of twisted trees, sagging ferns, and crumbling clay. You couldn't call the slope leading up to it a *hill* because a hill is something you could conceivably walk on — or something Julie Andrews could rustle to life with the sound of music. You couldn't call it a *precipice* because that's something solid enough to hurl yourself from. Maybe *embankment*. Parts of the slope are solid bedrock, but longer sections are a junkyard heap of landslides and somersaulting shrubs.

Dick confirms the price. "Oooooh," we sigh; the number of *o*'s commensurate with the price he's thrown out. And while it's beyond our budget, it's within our imaginations.

OUR PROPERTY

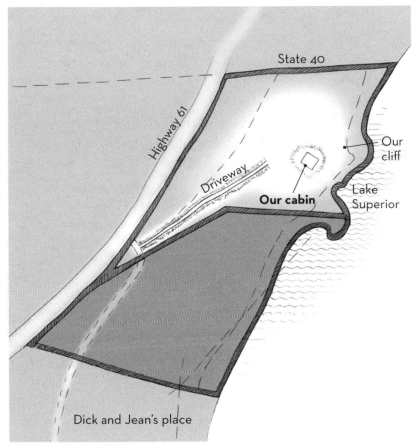

State 40

Highway 61

Driveway

Our cabin

Our cliff

Lake Superior

Dick and Jean's place

Dick and Jean Thorngren had purchased this thirty-eight acres of land with 3,500 feet of undulating Lake Superior shoreline in 1952 — the year I was born. Dick was nineteen. The area was called Kennedy's Landing. In 1952 land along Superior was purchased for work, not play. The previous owners had acquired it with the intention of starting a mink farm; the cool weather and close proximity to cheap fish made it a natural location. This was blue-collar land.

I've never asked Dick or Jean what they paid for the thirty-eight acres; surely they bought the entire chunk for a fraction of what they were asking for these little slices. But in 1952 the price was staggering. Payments on the land kept sucking them dry. Sucked them dry when their two daughters were born. Sucked them dry as they raised them in an 8-by-40-foot trailer for thirteen years. Sucked them dry as Jean used a propane torch to heat the water for their washing machine.

"There were times Jean and I didn't have two nickels to rub together," Dick later explained. "We couldn't afford to go to a movie. When it came time to clear the land, I couldn't afford a chain saw, so I cleared it with an axe."

Jean worked for twenty-six years in the office of Reserve Mining, the Valhalla-size taconite plant in Silver Bay. Dick worked construction, operated heavy machinery, and supervised projects. He traveled a lot. In between stints he built a ranch house down along the lake. In 1980 they opened a campground and put up with the highs and lows of thirty-nine campsites full of people — some with nothing but Coleman fuel between the ears. They put up with softball teams that put soggy cleats in their dryer at one in the morning, church groups that turned the shower house into a mud pit, and people who thought a KEEP OUT sign meant WALK RIGHT IN. Fifteen years later they took down the campground sign and officially retired.

A few years later they surveyed the land, divided it into six lots, and started selling off parcels seeded with fifty years of sweat, tears, and laughter. We were weighing two of them.

Dick jostles the F150 around in baby steps and drives up to the spot where we'd first grabbed the flyer describing the land many months ago. From the top down is the easiest access for exploring "the other" piece of land — this ugly sister, the piece of land we were destined to fall madly in love with. The land is so steep we have to hold on to branches with one hand, keep our balance with the other, and let our feet slide to descend. None of us is quite sure how we'll get back up. After a couple of hundred feet we hit a small flat spot.

Dick isn't a small man. He has the build of a man who's worked physically hard all his life, then let the muscle convert into, well, fish cakes. We turn around to see him completing the last part of the descent, wheezing, but standing. "I wish I could tell you two a little bit more about this land," he pants. "I've owned it forty-seven years but only stepped foot on it three times: twice to hunt and once to help survey it. It's just too damn hard to get around on." Our guess is that Dick has never been in sales.

Dick and Jean Thorngren, at home in their
rambler on Lake Superior

We stomp the land up and down: the uphill slope defined by Highway 61, the primary route between the Twin Cities and the Boundary Waters Canoe Area Wilderness and Canada. The lower slope ends in 340 feet of meandering shoreline. It's situated in a half-mile-wide cove labeled Crystal Bay on the survey, defined on each end by towering rock cliffs. In both directions we see the lake interacting with the shoreline. That's what we want: views of land and water meeting in all their calmness or ferocity, not endless horizon.

One part of the beach — the part we can't see from the point below — is a flat, pebbly area peppered with boulders. There are hundreds of birch trees and a small area where the land smoothe out to provide at least an imaginable building site. Below the site is a thumper hole — a small cave where, when the wind blows from the right direction, incoming waves compress and crash wildly outward. We hike the ravines, find the grown-over survey stakes, and hike the boundaries. The parcel of land directly next to it is a "State 40," forty acres of state-owned land so rugged and steep the chances of its being developed are nil.

Dick crab-walks his way back up the hill and leaves us alone. We pace out possible building sites, 3 feet to each of my strides, 2 feet to each of Kat's. We do this tongue-in-cheek, each of us waiting for the other to admit that the price simply doesn't jibe with the budget. And getting a driveway down that unwalkable slope — man, what will that cost? And a septic? And a well? We play chicken; neither of us swerves.

We hike the land so mesmerized that day turns into evening. We scramble our way back up the hill, then walk down to Dick and Jean's. We lay our naive financial situation on the line. Dick glances at Jean, gets some kind of silent signal only the long-married can give, then offers, "We can knock $10,000 off for getting the driveway in." A glass of water 10 inches beyond your reach doesn't quench your thirst any better than a glass 12 inches away, right?

We head out and creep north along Highway 61 to see two other pieces of land on our "to see" list. One is flat-out gorgeous with a million-dollar view and price tag to match. Another piece is affordable but swampy. We grab a room twenty miles up the shore and plot in that luxuriously impossible way people do when they first fall in love.

We go through the financial scenarios. Dick and Jean had said they'd carry a contract for deed if we could come up with a hefty down payment. I have money in an IRA we can cash in with a penalty. We have some savings and a few stocks. Kat can maybe finagle an advance out of the company she and her partner started two years before. We could try beating them up on price some more. We balance all this with the reality that we have five kids (some in college, some shortly headed that way), a house, and Kat's fledgling business.

The next day we head back to the land and explore every hill, cliff, and ravine. We try with little success to figure out how to get a driveway down the slope and how to scrunch a cabin, septic, and well in once we're there.

Dick suggests we call Bradley, an excavator from the town of Finland ten miles away. Brad fits every stereotype of an excavator: rough-and-tumble, fingers the size and color of hydraulic hoses, as sturdily built as the Cat 5 bulldozer he drives. We hike the land, scouting septic, building, and driveway sites. At one point the three of us are scrambling up a hopelessly steep and eroded part of the land. I'm in the lead, grabbing roots and finding footholds; Kat follows, and Brad brings up the rear. We reach a point where I've hoisted myself onto some flat land, but Kat's helplessly spinning her wheels. It becomes clear she's going down, taking Brad with her. Brad gives me a quick "a guy's gotta do what he's gotta do" glance, grabs Kat by the ass, and with one arm catapults her up the hill. Okay, here's a guy I can trust.

We ask Bradley for a rough estimate on the length of the driveway and what it would cost. He hems and haws. He has a couple of helpers start measuring the distance by extending a 100-foot tape, establishing a point, then pulling 100 more feet all the way down the hill. We press him again for a guesstimate, and again he stalls. He finally throws out "600, 700 feet."

His workers come panting back up the hill, huffing "325 feet." Kat and I glance at each other. Do we want an excavator who is 100 percent off on his estimates? A guy who would need to estimate slopes, angles, and fill? The answer turns out to be a resounding "yes." Bradley is honest to the penny and the most skilled — and, as we find out, ballsy — excavator around. Math just isn't his strong suit. But if I had to choose someone to pluck an apple off my head with a ten-ton backhoe, it would be Bradley.

We talk to one another, we talk to ourselves. Part of my thinking centers around how short a time my father enjoyed the cabin he and my mother bought years ago. They'd owned the cabin only a few months and slept there a handful of times before he died at the age of fifty-eight. If I follow my father's timetable I have ten years left — a fatalistic but not wholly unrealistic way of thinking. I also think about how fulfilling the hands-on building part could be. I'd worked as a carpenter for fifteen years but have worked the last ten as an editor for a home improvement magazine. I miss the solid whack of the hammer and the satisfied feeling of turning around at the end of the day to see real walls and a roof, not just another digital folder on the computer. Sawdust gets in your blood.

Kat's ruminating centers on other issues. The house we live in I'd built during my previous marriage. And though we've totally remodeled it, it still doesn't feel solidly hers. This cabin, regardless of how small, could be 100 percent, bona fide ours. Kat also loves a challenge — physical, financial, emotional — and this fits the bill.

We again walk over to Dick and Jean's with a list of questions. Water? They'd pumped theirs out of the lake and filtered it for decades. Septic? Well, we'd need a mound system, which could be expensive. Erosion? In the near-50 years they've owned the land, the lake and elements have claimed about 10 feet of hillside.

We drive to Bayfield, Wisconsin, hoping we might run across some levelheaded land to buy along the way. Driving the south shore of Superior, you hardly know you're skirting the same lake. Most of the land is pasture or farmland. For ninety percent of the drive you don't even see the lake. You don't encounter more of Superior's rugged grandeur until you approach Bayfield, a small harbor town that looks out over Madeline Island and the Apostle Islands. The town has a New England, hell-be-damned-if-you-like-us-or-not attitude. Fish boils (a food, not an infection) abound. Ramshackle buildings and converted warehouses shelter potters, painters, and a store that, at one point, sold nothing but olives.

The discussion along the way is nonstop land. In Bayfield we buy a six-pack of Coke, a bag of peanut M&Ms, and three cabin design books, then sit on a concrete breakwater paging through books and scenarios. It's one of those days when even full-tilt sun can't overtake the chill of Superior. Still we gab on. And we cross the line from impossible to semipossible.

We drive back home and rustle up our latest IRA statements. The hedonist in us whispers, "What's more important? A musty wad of money you'll spend on a Zip'r Roo Scooter and Depends in thirty years, or a cabin you can use right now?" We're careful not to tune in to any of Suze Orman's *How to Achieve Financial Independence* shows. We don't talk to friends or family because we know they'll talk us out of it. We arrive at our offer — an amount twice what we'd envisioned spending and that amount twice what we should have envisioned. It's an amount that would stretch us but an amount that, in the words of my father, we could "sleep with, accepted or rejected."

We make the call. Jean answers, and we present our offer. Dick is working in the pole barn 200 feet away; she chats via cordless phone as she walks over. We feel lumpy in the throat, like we're waiting for a "yes" or "no" for a prom date. Dick, as always, is up to his elbows in sawdust or grease and can't hold the phone. She hollers the offer to Dick, then, after a short pause, says, "He's nodding his head." Done.

Well, not quite.

II

DESIGNING
SMALL

You can't buy happiness by the square foot.

W HEN PEOPLE FIND WE'RE DESIGNING A CABIN, the questions
progress in a certain order.

"Where's the lot?"

"Seven miles north of Silver Bay, two miles beyond Palisade Head."

"What's the land like?"

"Three acres with manic-depressive shoreline, terrain like Everest, one almost-level spot the size of a basketball court."

"What kind of cabin will you build?"

"Small" is the only unqualified answer we can muster. If pressed for a style, we think something along the lines of "funky, seaside, carpenter-Gothic with Danish-style Arts and Crafts leanings" — a style you'd be hard pressed to find in any Architecture 101 book.

⸻

Cooks and designers have more in common than an insatiable appetite to star in their own reality TV shows. Those who cook create recipes; those who design create floor plans. Those who cook use ingredients; those who design use materials. And in both cases you find you can wind up with very different end products depending on how you combine the same fundamental materials. Victorian and ranch homes are both built with 2×4s; soufflés and scrambled eggs are both made with eggs. It just depends on how much of each ingredient you use, when you add it, what you combine it with, what spice you add, and how much care you take in the making. Good designers, like good chefs, snatch ingredients from different eras and disciplines.

So while "contemporary," "Queen Anne," "Craftsman," and "ranch" are all nice pigeonholes, few houses follow a style rigidly. "Victorian" isn't a style mandated in heaven but rather an evolving group of characteristics — turrets, bold colors, gingerbread millwork — that, by consensus, got a name hung on it. Surely there are pure examples of given architectural styles. Monticello is the essence of Greek Revival. The "painted ladies" of San Francisco scream Victorian. The houses of Levittown define the ranch style. But most houses are mutts.

So when we start designing Oma Tupa we don't start with a particular style but rather with a notion of what we like, need, and can afford. We want our cabin to be comfort food with an edge. We start doodling, borrowing an idea here and there, ripping pages out of magazines. Some of the design ideas are dictated by nature, as in, "Wow, we gotta frame that view with a gigantic window." Some are dictated by odds and ends we run into, as in, "Hey, Kat, there are some great old beams for sale cheap!" A design slowly evolves.

In his book *The Cabin,* architect and cabinologist Dale Mulfinger outlines what he feels are the minimum qualifications for a dwelling to be considered a cabin:

- **THE SITE IS CHOSEN FOR ITS NATURAL BEAUTY.**
  A cabin offers easy access to the outdoors, both through exterior rooms and through great views from the inside. A cabin adds to the land, never dominating it.
- **A CABIN PROVIDES SIMPLE, BASIC SHELTER.**
  It isn't fancy. It doesn't try to make a social statement, as houses often do. A small efficient floor plan is all it needs.

- **OVERLAPPING ACTIVITIES TAKE PLACE WITHIN THE COMPACT QUARTERS.** Thus a cabin promotes companionship and community spirit.
- **EVERYBODY FEELS AT HOME RIGHT AWAY.** A cabin's furnishings are simple, often treasured family hand-me-downs. Its sleeping lofts, tucked under the eaves, evoke memories of childhood. Its fireplace or woodstove provides physical and emotional warmth.

These words jibe with where we're headed. We have an awe-inspiring site. We want small. We want simple. We want comfortable.

In *Cabins* David and Jeanie Stiles extol: "The cabin is a simple, sacred place where food and drink always taste better, where music sounds brighter, where evenings with loved ones linger longer into pleasure, where sleep is deep and dawn is fresh with wonders we've elsewhere forgotten."

They got it right, too.

The average house built in the United States has 2,392 square feet. According to the National Association of Home Builders, that average house contains 13.97 tons of concrete, 13,127 board feet of framing lumber, 15 windows, 3 toilets and 3,100 square feet of shingles. There's plenty of space for everything and everybody. If you fight with your spouse you can go to your corners.

But not so with a cabin with a footprint of 440 square feet; 600 square feet when you throw in the loft. A 16-by-20-foot cabin is 2½ sheets of plywood running end to end and 4 sheets running side by side. It's a space you can cross the short way in five strides. Doors are at a premium because there's no place for them to swing. If you feud in a cabin that small, you've got no place to go. It's a marriage counselor made of drywall.

A 16-by-20-foot cabin is small — but not as small as we (or I should say *I*) had originally planned. The idea was to build something small and fast for starters — something that could later become a guesthouse. We'd build the real cabin later. The early doodles presumed a 12-by-12-foot cabin; a dwelling that could be built in a summer's worth of weekends. The kitchen was a Coleman stove, wet bar sink, and dorm-size refrigerator. The bathroom was a toilet, with the water heater and pressure tank stacked in one corner. The bathroom sink was the kitchen sink. There was a small loft, accessed by a ladder. There was one door and six windows.

At 144 square feet it was similar to the cabin Thoreau built in 1845 for $28.12. But while he only needed room for himself, a bed, a writing desk, and three chairs named Solitude, Friendship, and Society, our needs weren't quite as simple.

Kat was fine with the graph paper doodles of the 12-by-12-foot cabin. But when she took measuring tape and masking tape in hand and laid things out on our living room floor at home, her support of "small" got smaller. When she realized she'd nearly be able to load the woodstove from the toilet, the dissent began in earnest.

Freud, move over, because it was Kat's and my very different childhoods that forged our attitudes toward size. I grew up in a typical middle-class Minneapolis suburban house. I had my own bedroom. We had a single-car garage, a kitchen with a snack bar, and one and a half bathrooms — nothing ostentatious, but absolutely comfortable. Kat grew up in a family of exceedingly modest means in the less than bucolic town of Bemidji, Minnesota. The house she grew up in was one her father bought, then moved to the lot where it still stands and where her mother lived until a few years ago. For the first year water came from a hand pump beside the kitchen sink. Her bedroom was a compact attic shared with two sisters. The whole thing was perched on a bump-your-head-if-you-stand-up basement. Kat had had her fill of small and dark.

MAIN FLOOR PLAN

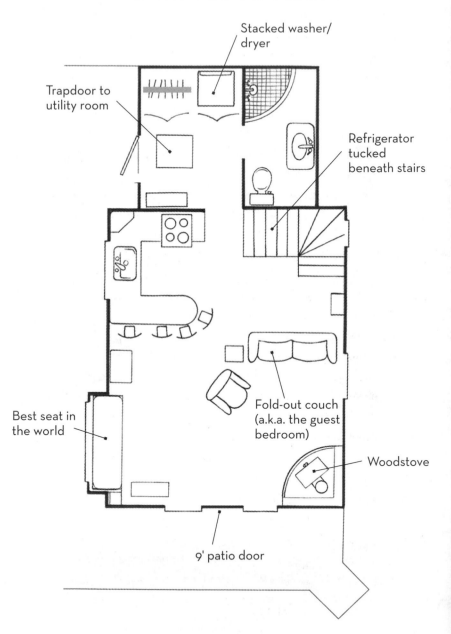

Stacked washer/
dryer

Trapdoor to
utility room

Refrigerator
tucked
beneath stairs

Best seat in
the world

Fold-out couch
(a.k.a. the guest
bedroom)

Woodstove

9' patio door

She had no intentions of going backward, and a cabin this small rang of reverse gear.

So we go up in size, working in 4-foot increments, because building materials work efficiently in 4-foot increments. We burn up the graph paper. We arrive at a size that's still compact but has more breathing room.

I tack together a bread box–size version of the cabin. We cut little windows out of cardboard and tape them here and there. Model cabin in hand, we stomp around the land positioning it in different places and orientations. I use a machete to thin out a few dozen small birches; at a landscaping center in the cities they'd have a price tag of $129 each. Funny how that works. Squinting helps us envision the views we'd have from each window and room. We set up a tall stepladder so we can try to picture the views from the loft. If we rotate the cabin clockwise we get a better view of the lake from the living room, but a worse view from the loft. If we move it away from the lake, the land becomes flatter and easier to build on, but hmmmm, that means we're farther from the lake. We tweak the design based on what we see and feel.

This is no small decision. This will be the first dwelling on this land. Ojibwe had lived in the area for over 600 years, but it's doubtful they would have built one of their birch-bark wigwams on this plot overlooking Gitchi (big) Gummi (water) — too damn steep. French explorers, trappers, and missionaries began roaming the area in the late 1600s, but if any of them had wanted to build a shelter, they would have stomped the quarter mile to the flat, sensible terrain of the old campground. Swedish and Norwegian immigrants began flocking to the area in the 1800s, but they too would have settled on land where their fishing boats and fishing sheds had easier access to the lake. The lumberjacks who arrived in the 1880s surely would have logged the 100-foot-tall white pine from the land, part of the 67 billion board feet of lumber harvested in Minnesota during the boom. And while the steep land would have made it easy to slide logs into Superior for the trip to the mill, the loggers would have rested their seesaw-weary bones in one of the logging camps near Beaver Bay. We were the first people unhinged enough to give it a whirl.

Designing the cabin is an ongoing process of give-and-take, of determining priorities, of trust, of love. Kat loves to cook, so the kitchen begins claiming more square footage. I need a mini-office for writing, so the loft grows a 4-foot leg for a desk. We love the lake views, so we incorporate a window seat, decks on two sides, and lots of windows. I like old wood and architectural antiques, so we keep the plan fluid enough to accommodate discoveries. We try to strike a balance between making good use of small nooks but not making it so space efficient it feels like a Winnebago.

The stairway drives much of the design. The 40 square feet it will occupy represents a whopping 10 percent of the floor space. The headroom in the loft will be low, making it impossible to position the stairway on an outside wall where the roof slopes down to meet the second

Kat with the foam board version of
Oma Tupa, Oma Lupa

floor knee walls. Placing it in the middle of the cabin will divide the already small space into two even smaller spaces. A ladder will take up only a quarter of the space, but looking to the future, we can't picture ourselves climbing a ladder with a cane in one hand and morning cup of coffee in the other. We doodle, erase, and rethink the overall plan — but the pencil just isn't sharp enough.

We raise the white flag and pay a visit to Katherine Hillbrand, an architect and interior designer with SALA Architects. We've loved working with Katherine on past projects because she has a knack for walking the line between solid design and whimsy. She thinks architecture should be fun. She has a way of adding a few unique details that turn a good design into a great one. Her mental search engine shows her right where to go with our stair problem. On the spot she breaks out her omnipresent roll of vellum paper and electric imagination and scratches out three good options.

The one we like most has an L-shaped stairway nestled along the bathroom wall with its final ascent paralleling that of the roof. There's not an inch of wasted space: A rollout pantry can tuck under the stairs next to a Lilliputian refrigerator. There's a little nook that could be turned into a coffee cup shelf. And look, there's a place on the landing for the round, stained glass parrot window impulsively bought at an antique store.

All the planning makes me drift back to the cabin my folks bought on Lake Waverly years before. Oma Tupa — when finished — will be the same size as theirs; both are perched on bodies of water; both are small and cozy. But they differ big time in terms of the neighborhood. The nearest dwelling to ours, Dick and Jean's house, will be a good 800 feet away. My parents' cabin was flanked on each side by cabins less than 15 feet away. The closeness did not play out well in their case.

On one side lived Gerold, whose hobby was building miniature cannons he entered in distance competitions with a Civil War reenactment group. He had a mini–smelting furnace situated on the property line where, on the weekends, he melted down disfigured plumbing pipe and old steering columns to make cannonballs for ammo. He tested his prototypes by picking off renegade cornstalks in the abandoned field across the road. Nothing like trying to relax not knowing when the next cannonball will rip overhead.

On the other side lived Marti and Rob; he, a three-pack-a-day grump, and she, a pathological chatterbox. She knocked on the door to chat five or six times a day. She kneweth no boundaries. When my folks sat out on the screen porch, Marti — from her screen porch — would start up conversations about milfoil weed and local traffic accidents. Sitting outside on a lounge chair became a non-option. One day, when my mother had absolutely had it, she inflated an air mattress and floated out into the middle of the lake to get away. Eyes shut, drifting on the water, she'd finally found peace and quiet at the cabin — until Marti paddled up on an air mattress, talking about the difficulties of finding good sewing patterns in a small town. My mother wondered wistfully if Gerold would ever lend out a cannon.

I'm glad we're flanked by Dick and Jean on one side and a State 40 on the other.

UPSTAIRS FLOOR PLAN

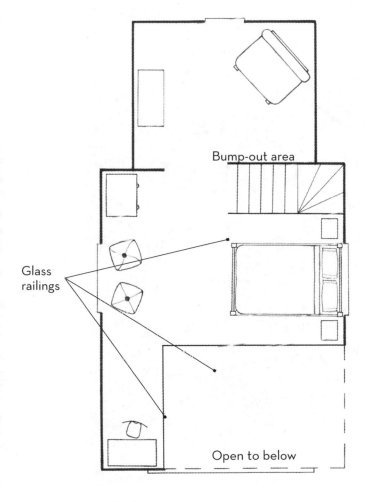

Bump-out area

Glass
railings

Open to below

Desk

THE RULES

Live a good life

When you build,
build with hands, head, and heart.

WE DON'T START WITH a written list of rules; nor do we end with one. We never post them anywhere, except the backs of our brains. We never refer to them as rule number such and such. There are no fines for breaking them; no sitting in the corner. Yet they hover. We use them to remind each other and ourselves that this cabin project is a slowing down, a shifting of gears, an adventure.

The rules are simple:

RULE 1: It's gotta be fun.

RULE 2: There's no hurry. We have forever, so let's do it right.

RULE 3: We decide everything together and do as much as we can together.

RULE 4: Hey, remember, it's gotta be fun. (See Rule #1.)

The first rule guides our minds; the second, our hands; the third, our hearts. And the fourth? Well, that's what the angel with a tool belt whispered in our ears when we got sidetracked. The rules got bent — in some cases annihilated — but they kept us moving in the right direction.

RULE #1: IT'S GOTTA BE FUN.

Kat and I are both hopelessly Scandinavian. Worse yet, Minnesota Scandinavian. We're most comfortable when we suffer. This trait was handed down by our Swedish and Norwegian ancestors, who endured depressing twenty-hour nights, only to be rewarded by sleep-deprived twenty-hour days. It comes from the cold that makes our blood run slower and from the frostbite that makes smiling painful. Minnesota has one of the largest populations of Scandinavians in the United States. The inclination toward hard work is embedded like a wood tick. Just as you hear tales of immigrant Swedes clearing forty acres with an axe and a three-legged ox, you'll find their modern-day counterpart snowblowing his driveway at one in the morning or hand-scraping every square inch of his house before repainting it.

Minnesotans' idea of fun is eating lutefisk — a dried cod soaked in lye — with in-laws. We endured Walter Mondale, a favorite son who won the electoral votes of only one state in the 1980 election — Minnesota. "Living on the edge" means driving onto a lake to ice fish after only three hard freezes. We golf on courses that are converted to ski hills come winter, snowmobile, and elect pro wrestlers for governor. We eat hot dish. We are hardened at a young age by waiting in 30-degrees-below-zero wind chills for snowbound school buses that never come. It's work for Minnesotans to have fun. So the "It's gotta be fun" attitude was not a natural act.

"Fun" should be loosely defined. When I was a rookie teacher in Denver, my mentor, a forty-five-year-old teacher and mother of seven, would respond to questions of policy or curriculum with, "If it's not fun, why do it?" Not necessarily a double over, split your seams kind of fun. Not a Chuckles the Clown "a little smile, a little prance, a little seltzer down your pants" kind of fun. No, her definition of fun meant approaching things with excitement, in the present, with a positive attitude and a sense of adventure. It was an expectation you would come out of the day a better person. Our expectation was to enjoy ourselves.

This all runs counter to our Monday through Friday city lives. Kat and I are co-CEOs of a large corporation — our family. When we merged in 1994, Kat brought Sarah and Kellie onto the board of trustees, and I brought Maggie, Zach, and Tessa. At points the Carlsen-Erickson Corporation has had four kids in college and a fleet of five vehicles with varying degrees of rust, mechanical fortitude, and insurance coverage. The corporate headquarters contained six bedrooms, nine telephones, six laptops, a fourteen-year-old Pekingese, and a psychotic cat. We managed the health, financial, and emotional needs of everyone as best we could. We couldn't fire anyone, though there were times we reached for the pink slips. There was — and continues to be — nothing more fulfilling, and nothing more exhausting, than raising a large family. So Rule #1 gets more than just lip service.

The clan perched in "the best seat in the world." Back row (l to r): Kat, Maggie, Kellie, Tessa. Front row (l to r): Spike, Sarah, Zach.

RULE #2: THERE'S NO HURRY.

"Taking our time" has two benefits: First, it takes away the pressure cooker that turns peace of mind into a pulp. Second, it provides the luxury of being able to do the job right. Kat and I both have jobs in which the above two constantly interplay: we work in fast-paced environments and have jobs that require precision.

Kat and her business partner, Troy, left a technical recruiting company several years ago to start their own business — PrimeStaff. When they left, the only things they carried out the door were grocery sacks of family pictures, a six-month no-compete clause, the ire of the owner, their reputations, and enough angst to kill a moose. They honored their no-compete clauses, rented a dinky office space, hung a shingle out, then spent two months of sleepless nights, staring at the ceiling, terrified that what they'd done was dumb, dumb, dumb, and irresponsible. Troy was looking at three kids under eight, and we were looking at five kids either in or headed toward college.

PrimeStaff is a technical recruiting firm that finds candidates for companies; sets up interviews; negotiates salary; arranges contracts; handles tax, medical, and worker comp deductions; and wrestles with personnel issues. At any given time they can have a hundred architects, engineers, surveyors, and interior designers on their payroll. The essence of a company like this is nonstop pressure.

When we started the cabin, I was the executive editor of *Family Handyman* magazine, a publication for do-it-yourselfers with a million subscribers and ten issues to crank out per year. The pressure came from the top (producing it) and bottom (making sure our readers loved it). We were always working on four or five issues in various stages of production. It was like juggling a feather, a cigarette lighter, and a bowling ball. There was rarely time to take time.

Yet on the flip side every article had to be absolutely, positively technically correct. Show the wrong wire under the wrong wire nut, and your readers get a circuit breaker that sparks rather than a light fixture that shines. Mislabel a "pipe wrench" as a "monkey wrench," and wait for the torrent of emails and letters from retired shop teachers. Get one letter wrong in a website address, and your readers are visiting Kinky's Massage rather than the ACME Window Supply.

Even in my previous lifetime as a builder and carpenter, I rarely had the luxury of time. Few clients savored cooking on hot plates and washing dishes in the bathtub while their kitchen was being remodeled. If you stripped half a roof of shingles, you had to keep laying new ones, even if it meant working until midnight with a headlamp strapped to your forehead. Some people have the romantic image of a carpenter, block plane in hand, coffee on the sawhorses, carefully cutting and fitting stairway parts to perfection. In fifteen years of carpentry, I only had two or three days that fit that romantic notion.

Take two high-stress jobs, then mix in five kids within seven years of one another, in various stages of academic success, heartbreak, college quandary, and driving skill, and some days we find ourselves tied to the railroad tracks, with the 10:15 coming and Dudley Do-Right nowhere in sight.

Rule #2 is the finger that reaches out and hits the **PAUSE** button. The cabin has no schedule. It doesn't need to be anywhere at a certain time. Here is something with a pace we can control.

RULE #3: WE DO AS MUCH AS WE CAN TOGETHER.

Getting a nettle in my toe made me realize Kat and I are only as strong as our weakest link — and we'll never know which link has the bad weld. It happened like this: Kat and I were walking on the perfect sand of a perfect Mexican beach on a perfect day. We had on sunscreen so we wouldn't burn, toted water so we wouldn't parch, and had cleared our heads so we wouldn't fret. We were walking to paradise. Then I stepped on a nettle, a thing so miniscule I could barely see it. It turned the day on its head. It made the journey back painful, turned the conversation we were having about the future into an obsession about an irritant in my middle toe. Rather than sail that afternoon I took Advil and lay in bed. And it was a metaphorical thing. It takes just one unpredictable thing happening — to Kat or me — to upset not just a walk, but a day, a year, or a lifetime. A single thing can — in a heartbeat, or lack of a heartbeat — dump all the perfection into the backseat. It happens all the time: Someone slips on the ice. A spot appears on an X-ray. A tornado flattens your life. And you can no longer do the things you love to do, and planned to do, as a couple. We gotta get while the gettin's good. It was an enlightening nettle.

So the cabin is an opportunity to not only build together but to plan together, drive together, browse through books for ideas together, shop together. Sometimes we make decisions solo, but the other person always holds veto power.

RULE #4: REMEMBER, YOU TWO: IT'S GOTTA BE FUN.

The last rule keeps us honest. It's easy to set up a game plan, then let it slip away. We keep our fun radar tuned in, and when the early warning signs appear — using four-letter words to describe paint cans, tripping over brooms, forgetting a measurement in the time it takes to walk 3 feet — we say, "Screw it." We walk the shoreline, play gin, fool around, visit Dick and Jean, take a nap. Because those are the rules.

IV

PAPERWORK & EARTHWORKS

Mensch tracht, Gott lacht.
(Man plans, God laughs.)

—*Yiddish proverb*

F INALIZING THE PURCHASE DETAILS with Dick and Jean takes
two minutes, four signatures, four handshakes, and two Kat hugs.
Dick closes the agreement with, "Now remember, if you kids ever have
trouble making your payment, just come talk to us. We like you guys.
Things happen. So if you have a problem, you just come talk to us." This
is not an empty offer. He means it. Dick means everything he says —
you know straight up where you stand with him.

But before we can legally close we need to wade through murky
"legal title" waters. The St. Paul lawyer we hire to do the title search —
a process to ensure the land has clear title from its first owner up to
the most recent — eventually gives up. "You better hire a local guy who
knows how to negotiate the land mines up there," he mutters.

The first call from our second lawyer, our North Shore lawyer, starts
with, "You know, no one *really* owns land in the United States . . . ," words
that have the unmistakable stickiness of red tape. The land is entangled
in an Act of Congress dated February 26, 1857, a year before Minnesota
was admitted into the Union. Our forefathers — wisely, but with no
sensitivity to the fact it would cost us, Spike and Kat Carlsen, a chunk
in lawyers' fees 150 years later — set aside "sections numbered sixteen
and thirty-six in every township of public lands in said state," to "be
granted to said state for the use of schools." In short, the state could

build a school on those sections or sell them to pay for schools. Our land sat firmly within section thirty-six. It seems ridiculous that ownership is in question after a century and a half, but lawyers deal with the ridiculous for a living. It finally takes verification from the Bureau of Land Management in Springfield, Virginia, to clear up that part of the title.

The lawyer wades through the forty-two entries in the Abstract of Title — a skinny booklet logging all the transactions, subdivisions, and permits connected to our parcel of land. He finds no delinquent taxes, judgments, or indications of hazardous wastes. He finds easements for the telephone and power companies and the highway department — all perfectly normal and all nipping around the heels of the notion that no one *really* owns land in the United States.

There are more fits and starts. The abstract gets lost in transit between the big-city and small-city lawyers. They have to track down a descendant of a previous owner out in Montana to sign some release papers. Finally the title is clear enough to make the transaction official. We take the next step – getting permits to build.

Obtaining a permit to build a house in some areas can be as painful as yanking a fishhook out of your eyelid. Every community has a different legal maze to negotiate. In most cases you initiate the process by submitting a complete set of blueprints to the local building department. These plans illustrate and specify details right down to the thickness of the roof sheathing and length of the fasteners used to secure it. It shows detailed cutaway sections of walls — working through drywall, vapor barrier, insulation, framing and sheathing materials, house wrap, siding, and exterior finish. There are various views that look like the hand of God has taken the roof off or used a large circular saw to cut through the center of the house to reveal its innards. There are often separate plumbing, electrical, and HVAC (heating, ventilation, and air conditioning) plans.

Once an inspector okays the plans, you purchase a building permit; the cost is contingent on the size and value of the structure. The permit for a typical $200,000 new structure in a typical community is about a grand — and as the value of your project rises, so does the price of the permit.

In most communities you need to have the work inspected at various stages. There's a footing inspection to make sure the concrete footings you're about to pour are on your property, deep enough, and on solid, undisturbed earth. You need a rough framing inspection to make sure the studs, joists, and rafters are beefy enough, numerous enough, and secured according to plan; that the plumber hasn't cut a 6-inch hole through an 8-inch joist. You need a plumbing inspection to verify there are no leaks and everything is vented and flowing in the right direction. You need an insulation inspection — a step instituted during the 1980s energy crisis — to make sure the fiberglass and vapor barrier are installed right. In some micromanaged areas you even need a "drywall fastener" inspection to ensure you use the right nails or screws and that they're spaced properly.

And you need a final inspection to make sure the stair railings are installed at the right height (34 to 38 inches above the nose of the tread, please), the firewall between garage and house is the right thickness (5/8-inch drywall so a garage fire won't spread as fast), and all the bedrooms have egress windows (a minimum of a 20 by 24-inch clear opening, within 44 inches of the floor, so the average firefighter with an average air tank on his or her back can crawl in to rescue the average occupant). Plus lots more.

Some communities take purity of design a step further with "protective covenants" — an extra layer of rules imposed to maintain a certain look. Some developments have minimum square-footage requirements and mandate triple garages, a way of saying, "No boats, rusted teenagers' cars, or lawn tractors in the driveway, pul-l-l-l-lease!" Some communities specify a limited palette of colors from which you may choose to paint the exterior of your home. One quaint community, Seaside, in the Florida Panhandle, has covenants dictating all houses have front porches and white picket fences, of which no two can be the same on the same street. Kat and I stayed at a bed-and-breakfast in a community that dictated that every house look at least 200 years old from the outside. At least one snooty community has a protective covenant that limits the number of dogs or cats a household can have to two.

My impression is that Oma Tupa — perched along Lake Superior, abutting state property and in the heart of vacationland — will be infested with covenants, permit requirements, and inspections. When I call the county offices, I'm told not only are there no protective covenants, there's no building inspector. We need only a "Land Use" permit. When I ask what that involves, the clerk says, "Well, you give Walt a call, ya stomp around the land with him to make sure everything fits, and then he gives you a permit."

It sounds easy, and is. The Land Use application is one and a half pages long — microscopic by bureaucratic standards. The other papers Walt brings list a few sensible requirements. There needs to be a "perc test" — to make sure the wastewater can percolate adequately into the ground — before installing the septic system. Our septic system has to be 50 feet from our well to minimize the chance that bacteria will leach into the groundwater. We're so unsure of our financial wherewithal that we sign a "sewage treatment system exemption," which gives us the right to use a portable toilet for the first year.

If the Building Codes Gods were to select just one regulation to enforce, the one I would lobby for hardest would be the septic regulations. Cabins used to be different animals. Not that long ago waste management meant putting a match to your garbage on a calm day, pest control involved picking up your shotgun, and sewage systems looked an awful lot like a shovel and a Sears catalog. Cabins were just a dot here and there along the lakeshore, and not that frequently visited. Sewage disposal wasn't much of an issue. Mother Nature had plenty of give.

But then shacks that used to be seasonal cabins became year-round lake homes, and more and more dots appeared on the maps, and with the dots came people, and with the people came their sewage. Even those cabins that had advanced beyond the outhouse stage often had no more than a holding tank with an overflow pipe shooting into the lake.

Lake Waverly, where my folks had their cabin, literally turned green over the course of a few years from all the nitrates that slunk from toilet to lake. That, combined with the fertilizer people applied to their lawns — lawns that sloped down to the lake — made the lake unswimmable, unboatable, and, eventually, unfishable because of the proliferation of algae and seaweed and lack of oxygen. It required sewer lines, a waste treatment facility, a ginormous federal grant, and years for the lake to recover. It's still recovering. I'm all for tip-top shape septic systems.

There are vague property setback requirements. Our dwelling needs to be 20 feet from the property lines on either side, 35 feet from the highway right-of-way, and 65 feet from the "vegetation line" of Lake Superior. We can't pry a good definition of *vegetation line* from anyone. Does it mean 65 feet from the closest living plant along the shoreline? Does it mean from the biggest permanent plant, like a tree? Does lichen count? Was this 65 feet as the crow flies or as the land slopes? When I press one official by telling him we want to build as close to the lake as possible, he looks at me with a wry grin and says, "Yeah, well, that's why most people buy lakeshore. I doubt anyone's ever gonna go down there with a tape measure." We soon discover the area favors a "don't ask, don't tell" philosophy. As long as you aren't blatant about things, as long as you don't piss off your neighbors, as long as you're respectful, reasonable, and responsible, it's okay.

We close on the land in August. To me that seems enough work for the year; we should ponder design, schedule, and finances over the winter. Kat has other ideas. She sees no reason we shouldn't get the driveway in now, so we can dive and drive right in come spring.

This is one of the areas where Kat and I are different. I'm inclined to dawdle in matters of planning. Kat, on the other hand, just sprints. If I'm coal powered, Kat is nuclear. She has what physicists call "a vast storehouse of potential energy." It's a power source not apparent on the surface, an energy with a complicated source, an energy that's seemingly inexhaustible. So the land, that to my way of thinking was to lie sleepy and fallow over the winter, is given a hotfoot.

Bradley builds the driveway. The task requires hauling in twenty truckloads of fill — 300 tons more or less — to create a level ribbon of driveway as it crawls diagonally down the embankment. It requires dumping a load, smoothing it with the dozer, compacting it, moving 10 feet down the newly created ramp, then repeating this process. He hauls in truckloads of boulders weighing up to five tons each, to stabilize the edge of the driveway. I ride along with him to pick up one load, and when we get to the top of the driveway, he turns to me and raises the hair on the back of my neck by growling, "Hey, why don't you back 'er down?" We're awed by Bradley and his machines, and their ability to turn what was an unwalkable slope into a drivable driveway.

Things snowball according to the "as long as" principle. It only makes sense for Bradley to dig a 4-foot-deep trench along the driveway as long as he's there so the power and phone companies can drop their underground lines in. And as long as he's at the bottom of the hill, we might as well have him put the septic system in. And as long as he's still there he might as well clear a little spot for the cabin. And as long as we have a power cable running down the hill, we might as well mount a meter and outlet on a pole and have the power company hook us up to the grid, right? And as long as the land is cleared and there is a driveway and electricity, well, gosh, maybe we should have a load of lumber delivered so we'd be all set to go in the spring. Well, sheeee-it, as long as that lumber is there, we might as well start on that cabin, eh?

Kat and I aren't hard-core environmentalists — we aren't out there marking every anthill and seedling to protect them during excavation. We don't apologize to each tree as we rev up the chain saw. But we do intend to tread gently on the land. We use yellow ribbons to mark the trees we want Bradley to take out when he clears the small section for the cabin. There aren't many; we want trees tightly surrounding the

I celebrate the near-completion of the driveway by doing the
"I love my Toyota" jump (even though the truck is a Dodge).

cabin and the sound of rustling leaves. Bradley takes out the ones we mark — plus another dozen. "Yah, they may look nice, but wait until one crashes through your skylight in an ice storm."

Bradley is excavator, land planner, and fortune-teller rolled into one. When I ask him to dump a load of boulders so I can build a retaining wall along the back of the cabin, he just builds it. I wanted artsy-fartsy, aesthetically stacked rocks; Brad wanted done. Besides, his idea of a "boulder" differed drastically from mine. In my mind they were bowling ball–size stones I could stack by hand. In Bradley's mind (and dump truck) they were the size of *Tyrannosaurus rex* skulls. Again he's right; what would have taken me a week and a five-gallon bucket of Advil to build he built in an hour. The wall isn't something you'll see in *Landscaping Today*, but it'll hold back a glacier when the next ice age comes.

━━━━

We want the septic on the south side of the cabin, but Bradley puts it on the north. "Won't be in your way when you decide to add on." Again he's right. We would have lost all flexibility.

Bradley makes other executive decisions when it comes to the septic. Septic systems have two main parts: The first is a 1,500-gallon or larger concrete holding tank into which everything — dishwater, bodily waste, shower water, contact lenses — drains. Inside that tank the solids settle to the bottom and are aptly named "sludge." Solids constitute a small amount of what goes into the tank, and bacterial action decomposes things even further. At the end of the day — actually, the end of the year — there isn't much sludge. Grease, oil, and fats rise to the top of the tank to create the scum layer. Every year or two the "honey truck" comes and pumps out the sludge, scum, and effluent in between.

The second part of the system consists of a leach field — a series of perforated pipes and gravel-filled trenches where the fluids from the tank flow, eventually to percolate into the ground and evaporate. The entire system runs on gravity, no batteries required. The size of a septic system is based on the number of bedrooms in a home; the more occupants, the more waste. On the septic permit they don't ask you how much you eat, the size of your bladder, or how many showers you take a day. They want number of bedrooms.

In sandy or well-drained soils a contractor digs a few trenches, fills them with gravel, installs a few hundred feet of perforated plastic pipe and connects this labyrinth to the holding tank. There are pipes sticking up here and there for cleaning the system out. The fluids mosey through the field and dissipate. But the more clay or solid rock in an area, the harder it is for the fluids to dissipate. And in really rocky and clayey areas you need to actually create an area of porous ground by bringing in mounds of gravel and sand. This system is, no surprise, called a mound system. Many, many dwellings along the North Shore have one, and they can be wickedly expensive. The thrill of owning one is on par with the thrill of buying new tires or getting a hip replacement — no one notices, but they're a necessity.

The final decision as to what type and size of leach field to install — conventional or mound — rests on the results of the percolation or "perc" test, which determines how quickly fluids can percolate, or soak, into the soil. The test involves a fairly archaic procedure. The contractor bores a series of holes, fills them with water to a specified depth, then times how long it takes the water to dissipate. Fast is good. The results of this test determine the size and type of leach field you need to install.

Brad's wife is certified to conduct these tests. She and Bradley spent what I could only imagine to be a pastoral afternoon, digging holes around our 3 acres and doing perc tests. About 100 feet behind and above the cabin they find soil that drains like a colander. The only thing this location has going against it is gravity, since it's uphill from the cabin. This principle of physics could be defied by installing a pump in the tank that would lift the fluids to the area. A $900 pump could save us the extra five to ten grand a mound system would cost us.

Good-draining soil in that neck of the woods is unheard of. This is God's hand slipping a stack of one-hundred-dollar bills into our mythical bank account. Later we surmise this is no act of God but rather a long-ago act of the highway department. The old highway, built from tons and tons of good-percolating sand and gravel that had been hauled in, ran right close to this miraculous leach field. You gotta grab good luck when it sails by.

A septic tank without water is an unemployed septic tank. So we begin pondering the aquatic half of the equation. The obvious approach is to drill a well. But having asked around, we discover it's an iffy proposition, with a high probability of striking brackish water. In our area three quadrillion gallons of fresh water may be sitting 100 feet beyond us, but drill 200 feet down and we'll most likely tap into an aquifer or "lens" of salty water, two billion years in the making; part of what geologists call the Canadian Shield. But it's worth talking to a driller or two to make an informed decision.

One driller hops out of the cab of his truck brandishing a wishbone-shaped birch branch. "It's a witching stick," he explains. The skeptic in me looms large as he holds the two legs of the stick tightly in his hands and begins walking around. The skeptic in me starts stomping up and down when the free end of the stick rotates and points straight down.

"There's your water," he says with absolute certainty, marking the spot with his hat.

Aaah, now the Brooklyn Bridge I purchased can have water running under it.

The curious side of me asks him if I can try his stick. I grasp the two legs as tightly as I can and start witching at a point 20 feet away from his "there's-your-water" spot. At the exact point he's marked, the stick begins to point downward. I give the stick my antisupernatural death grip. It's unstoppable. I walk around the area again — this time with my eyes shut to eliminate the chance that a brain fart is in command. Once more the tip churns downward. Hmm.

Turns out, even some of the most high-tech, million-dollar drilling rigs have a willow branch in the toolbox to dowse for water. In the '60s the U. S. Marines tried dowsing to locate tunnels and weapons stashes in Vietnam, and in 1986 when thirty soldiers were buried in an avalanche during a NATO exercise, Norwegian soldiers broke out the divining rods.

But the driller didn't need a witching stick to point out the overhead high-voltage transmission lines we'd need to move to get the drilling rig down the driveway or the rock we'd need to dynamite to get a trench deep enough to bury the waterline to the cabin. His divining rod couldn't tell us how deep down the water was and whether or not it would be brackish. No divining rod was required to determine our checkbook was no gusher.

We need running water but want something more sophisticated than Kat and me running to get it. So we look toward a sure source — the lake. If we could get a waterline from point A to point B we know we'd never be out of water. We'll need to make that decision soon, but right now we're more excited about making sawdust.

V

A _Solid_ FOUNDATION

When you dig a hole,
be smarter than the shovel.

D ON'T LET THE NONAMBULATORY STATE of a cabin mislead you; it's
a living thing. The 100-amp electrical service panel is the brain;
the wires are the nerve fibers; the outlets, switches, and lights are the
nerve endings. The hot and cold water pipes are the veins that nourish.
The drain, waste, and vent pipes create the intestines that usher the
waste away; the cabin is actually superior to us since it expels gas up
and through a roof vent, versus humanity's lower trajectory. The shingles are the hair, the siding and insulation are the skin, the paint is the
makeup, the heating system is the lungs, and the rough framework is the
skeleton. But you need to start from the ground up. With a cabin, as with
any entity, you need to begin with solid feet and legs — the foundation.

There are two approaches we can take to building on a steep slope. The
first is setting the cabin on a full basement; one where the backside
would be buried 6 or 7 feet and the front or downhill side exposed. This
approach would involve dozing a mammoth wedge of soil out of the
earth to create a flat subterranean surface. The upside is we could create both a foundation and usable square footage beneath the cabin. The
downside is it would rearrange both our budget and the landscape in a
serious way.

The second option is the "stork" approach. The cabin would perch on a rectangular grid of legs or wood posts; taller ones on the downhill side, shorter ones on the uphill. It would be an inexpensive, low-impact way of building. We wouldn't need a twenty-ton bulldozer rearranging the earth, only a twelve-pound posthole digger. Posts would allow us to leave the slope of the ground basically unaltered and to tread more gently on the land. And posts would allow us to build quickly and inexpensively.

We go with the stork option, eyes wide open about the drawbacks. With post footings on a steep slope, we realize we will give up the basement to store tools and obnoxious relatives. We're committing ourselves to hard, tedious handwork — a solid chunk of blood, sweat, and tears.

To support our 16-by-20-foot cabin we need nine posts — three rows of three — plus two more posts to support the small bump-out on the back. We also need posts to support the front deck, bringing the grand total to fourteen. We run strings between stakes to indicate the perimeter of the cabin, then pound in stakes to mark where each post will go. Time to dig in.

The hierarchy of soil dig-ability goes as thus:

- **EASIEST**: Sand and dirt. They're homogeneous, predictable, and light.
- **HARD**: Soil with lots of tree roots, especially those so beefy you can't chop through them with a shovel. Especially if the roots are so gnarly and ill-tempered you need to be a contortionist with a reciprocating saw to get rid of them.
- **HARDER**: Soils with lots of clay; heavy, dense, sticky clay that clings to your shovel or posthole digger like a campfire marshmallow. You spend as much time scraping gumbo off your shovel as actually digging.

- **HARDEST**: Soils with rocks of all sizes. Small rocks throw your posthole digger off course, medium-size rocks dull it, and large rocks break it.
- **HARDLY WORTH ATTEMPTING**: Clayey soil, with roots and rocks; the soil we encounter.

After spending 3 hours digging the first hole by hand — 16 inches in diameter, 54 inches deep — I calculate I will spend 42 hours on this task alone. This is *Cool Hand Luke* work. It's not the way I want to spend an entire week. I need to be smarter than the shovel.

A gas-powered auger ain't gonna cut it. We need a machine. Bradley is booked, so I find the only other excavator in the area who has a Bobcat skid loader with a hole auger attachment. He agrees to meet me at the site at five o'clock, after his day job. I recheck and restake the location of each hole as I wait. It's fall, and the temperature drops to 40 as the sun sets. Seven p.m. and still no auger. There's no cell phone reception, and I figure he's been waylaid. I'm chilled to the bone and start packing up when I see headlights and a trailer bouncing down the driveway.

"Decided to do 'er tomorrow, eh?" I say, using a tone sarcastic enough to show my displeasure, yet friendly enough to not alienate the only guy within 100 miles who can get this godforsaken job done.

"Hell, no. I got headlights!" he says as he fires up the machine.

And soon it becomes clear this is not a one-man operation. He sits bobbling on his Bobcat while I, under the glare of headlights, use a shovel and pickaxe to pry and chop the sticky clay off the auger after each plunge. I use a clam digger–type posthole digger to try to lift loose rocks out of the bottoms of the holes when they fall in. Most of the time I'm on my knees. My pants and shirt are soaked, half from sweat and half from the sodden soil flying through the air. We're working on a slope, so I hand-guide the auger to vertical before each plunge; I'm hoping he's packed plenty of tourniquets for when this thing rips both my arms off. I spend three hours, frozen, wet, and bone weary genuflecting to the auger god.

I'm paying him; isn't something wrong here? No, if I were on the Bobcat it would be a submarine on the bottom of Superior. Both hands and both feet are required to drive, steer, lift, and dump the Bobcat and auger in a coordinated effort. A good Bobcat operator is part excavator, part ballet dancer; Baryshnikov in a hard hat. By the time we're done, it's pitch black. I'm soaked, caked in clay, nearly deaf from the noise, and sleep deprived — but hey, look at those fourteen holes. Beauty is in the eyes of the beholder — especially if the beholder just dodged five days of brutal work.

I ask what I owe him, and he responds, "Well, what's it worth to you?" And while the correct answer is, "My firstborn son and ten thousand dollars," we settle on a more reasonable two hundred bucks.

The support posts need to sit on concrete pads. Mixing concrete requires water, and there's plenty of that around — it's just 200 feet down a 60-degree cliff. We buy three old five-gallon plastic jerry cans at a garage sale, and Kat and I start hauling. To fill the jugs we kneel on jagged rock and force them underwater, using the muscle mechanics you'd use drowning a hippo. We tie ropes from tree to tree, and as we ascend, one-handed, with the forty-pound jugs, we slip, slide, grunt, and struggle to keep our footing. This is how people wind up in the "News of the Weird" column. It's not how two reasonably intelligent people get water from point A to point B. It would be more reasonable to buy twelve-ounce bottles of Perrier from the gift shop up the road.

On our third trip up the hill we encounter Dick standing at the top. We've known Dick long enough to be able to judge his mood, even before he says something, based on the direction and velocity of his jowls. You do not want to see rapid horizontal movement. But they're moving vertically, and he's got a big grin.

We're wheezing, with high-water pants and burrs stuck to our socks. "Now ain't that somethin'," he hoots — the phrase he utters when he doesn't know what else to say or is reloading for his next quip.

"You know we got a garden hose, and you got a truck. I bet we could figure out a better way to do that."

Yah, ain't that somethin'.

Visitors are surprised to see the cabin perched on nine modest-size posts. Each is made from three "foundation grade" treated 2×6s nailed together, making each post 4½ by 5½ inches in cross section. Not that massive. But wood is incredibly strong in the vertical position, much stronger than it is lying flat or lying on edge. A single vertical 2×6, prevented from bending, can support fifteen tons before reaching its limits. That means each post can theoretically support forty-five tons, and as a group can support more than 400 tons' worth of cabin.

When we dig the holes, the cabin still looks small on paper. One or two bags of concrete in each hole will support the posts that will support the beams that will support the joists that will support the walls that will support the roof. There can be no weak link in this chain of command.

We get the concrete pads poured and the posts positioned and backfilled. I step back and squint, trying to picture the cabin with all its parts, occupants, furnishings, and snowloads. But instead of hearing a deep, booming voice say, "And it was good," I hear a scrawny little inner voice asking, "Don't you think nine posts and fifteen bags of concrete are a wee bit on the light side?"

Yet getting the foundation in — whether it consists of nine posts or fifty tons of concrete for a poured basement — is a milestone in cold

FOUNDATION FOOTPRINT

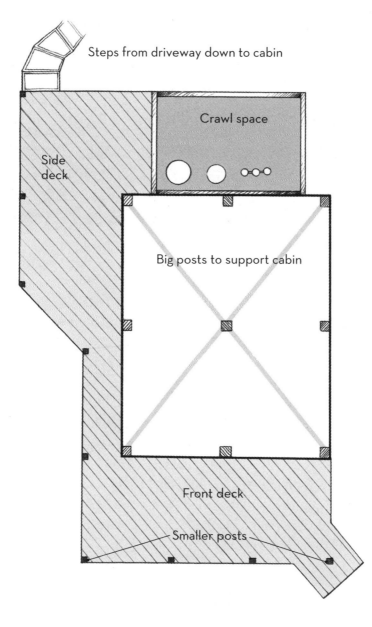

Steps from driveway down to cabin

Crawl space

Side deck

Big posts to support cabin

Front deck

Smaller posts

I stand amid the grid of posts and beams that form the foundation of the cabin. The posts for the ill-fated bump-out are in the foreground.

climates. It means you're up and out of the frozen soil and can keep building through the rest of the winter. If you're crazy enough.

It's early October, and Kat comes up to help frame the floor. I am in dire need of her companionship, energy, and enthusiasm.

We build the four perimeter beams and the beam down the middle for the floor. Each is built from three 2×12s nailed together and secured to the posts. Normally the lumber used for a floor would be everyday H/F (hemlock-fir) or S/P/F (spruce-pine-fir). But we're so unsure how long it will take us to build the cabin, we use pressure-treated wood in case the floor framework is exposed to the elements too long.

One of the beauties of carpentry is the way pure theoretical math and the savagery of a swinging hammer merge. You build the perimeter of the floor to the exact dimensions. You square it up by measuring diagonally corner to corner in both directions. You whack the framework with a sledgehammer until these diagonal measurements are identical. You brace the posts — or at least should brace the posts — so they don't move. You lay out the positions of the joists every 12, 16, or 24 inches. And if you've done your legwork and headwork right, all the joists are the same length, the batts of insulation that rest between the joists fit snug, the ends of each sheet of plywood for the floor break in the middle of a joist. The tongues fit tightly in the grooves as you whack the sheets of plywood together. And things work just that way. I'm Pythagoras, and Kat is Archimedes. The weekend brings perfect fall days with crisp sun, crisp air, and a crisp sense of well-being.

We build the deck along the front of the cabin so we have a place to work from and store materials. It's during this time Kat begins wearing her tool belt and hammer with a certain swagger. Tool belts are a true rite of passage. Rookies don't wear them and waste hours fetching tools and nails scattered here and there; they're on a ladder ready to install part X but, whoops, their hammer is over there under part Z. A belt keeps everything where you need it. Carpenters grow to love their tool belts like kids do their favorite binkies and blankies. It's comforting. You get to know every stitch and flaw. The hand goes automatically to the pencil, the speed square, the nail pouch, the tape measure. It's the gunslinger's holster, and the hand draws the hammer as smoothly as Billy the Kid drew his pistol. One carpenter I worked with would signal the end of each lunch break with, "I better put on my tool belt so I can think," and there's some truth to it. Kat's tool belt is beginning to mold around her.

Hammers also become sentimental things to carpenters, and Kat is no exception — she adopts one from my arsenal of tools. The old saw goes,

"I've used the same hammer thirty years — only had to replace the handle three times and the head twice." She's getting it all down. Once she learns to dig out slivers from her hand with the utility knife, she'll earn her place in the fraternal order of carpenters.

We install the posts and joists for the small bump-out in the back but don't sheathe it with plywood. There's something unsettlingly small about it. This is where a small refrigerator, a microwave, a sink, and a few cabinets to hold a weekend's worth of food will sit. Kat has a vision of cooking bread and soup on lazy fall days, and this is not a lazy-fall-day kitchen. It is all work and no play. It faces away from the lake. It's more of a compartment than a kitchen.

Cooking and breaking bread with family and friends is one of the main activities of cabin living. In *The Seasonal Cabin Cookbook* Teresa Marrone muses, "Cabin life runs on a different pace than everyday life. Because you're free of the 9-to-5 schedule of the workaday world, your routines are likely to be less structured. Breakfast doesn't have to be a bagel-and-coffee over the kitchen sink at 7:45 while waiting for the carpool. Lunch isn't just the event that occurs between 11:45 and 12:45. Dinner doesn't have to be orchestrated to sandwich between the end of the kids' soccer practice and the start of the evening aerobics class at the gym. At the cabin, you can kick back and watch a loon dive for its breakfast, pack a picnic lunch to take on a hike and enjoy a leisurely dinner while watching the sunset."

It's clear the kitchen part of the design is ill fated. I begin to look at the kitchen bump-out the same way I do a bad paragraph: a lot of work has gone into it, it's done, but it just doesn't work. The wise option is to throw it out and start over. And sometimes it takes an editor to tell you this, even though you know it's true. Kat is the editor on this one. We hold off doing anything more to the bump-out.

We finish framing and sheathing the floor for the rest of the cabin. It's late October, and we know we're fiddling with fate by trying to push the project much further. Rather than risk standing a few walls and having them buffeted by Superior's gales and snows over the winter, we cover the floor and call it a year. A 16-by-20-foot, blue polyethylene tarp does the job.

We step back and take a look at our creation. We're all smiley and puffy chested, when once again I hear that ethereal internal voice again, questioning. "What makes you so cocksure you didn't build too close to that bumbling cliff?" The most irreversible building mistake a person can make is to put a structure in harm's way. It only takes a film clip on the ten o'clock news showing a four-million-dollar house sliding down the hills of Laguna Beach or a modular home bobbing down the Grand Fork River to realize bad judgment abounds in places other than your teen's head. Maybe someday Oma Tupa will be on that ten o'clock newsreel. But dammit, at least for now we got proximity; we got a *view*.

It's a good thing we hold off completing the floor for the kitchen bump-out, because the next spring we take pry bars and sledge hammers and dismantle it. Over a winter's worth of doodling and discussing, we realize that if we expand the space to 6 by 12 feet, we can shoehorn a bathroom, a closet, and an entry into this space, opening up more room for a kitchen in the main part of the cabin. As a bonus we could include a crawl space where we could house the water heater, filters, and pressure tank. And for the daily double we could create a loft in the upper reaches of the bump-out; a fortlike space big enough to bunk future grandkids. We have Bradley come in with his backhoe to dig a four-foot-deep pit to accommodate a crawl space for the larger bump-out.

A wood foundation makes the most sense, since we can use gravel for the footings and build the crawl space walls ourselves. Kat and I hand-level the pit, start spreading the gravel shovelful by shovelful, and look at each other. Hell, let's not let the good stand in the way of the great; let's kick it up a notch. With pickaxes and shovels we excavate the pit so we can increase the size to 10 by 12 feet.

We're working in the muck. It's April and 40 degrees, warm enough so we sweat when we work and cold enough to freeze when we stop. The mudflies are hatching, and we're the nearest food. But the pure physicality of it all is refreshing. We dig a little, fill the wheelbarrow with gravel, dump it into the pit, spread it, then repeat. Over and over and over. No decisions to make. Bliss — until we hit a rock. We can't divine how big this subterranean boulder is until we start whittling around the edges. After thirty minutes we realize this is the Orson Welles of boulders; absolutely massive. We ponder whether we should reduce the size of the bump-out or call Bradley. We make the call. He cruises down, jumps on his backhoe parked nearby, claws the megarock out in three minutes, smooths the bottom of the pit in three swipes, dumps the rest of the gravel in the pit with a few trips of the bucket, and heads back up the hill, all in fifteen minutes — and that includes five minutes of BS-ing. He could have done in twenty minutes what it's taken us all day to do by hand.

We work a few more hours, grow weary, then perk up at the sound we love to hear — two four-wheel ATVs coming down the driveway. It's Dick and Jean. They bestow upon us a paper plate piled high with piping hot fish cakes and three rib-cracking Ole and Lena jokes. Ain't that somethin'?

———

Kat leaves to man the home front. I build the four crawl space walls from lumber and plywood that's been pressure treated to withstand moisture, insects, and fungi attack. I whack the studs together, sheathe them with plywood, and secure them to 2-by-8-foot pressure-treated footing plates leveled into the gravel.

At first glance using wood for an underground crawl space appears, well, stupid. But tests by the Forest Products Laboratory show otherwise. In 1938 scientists from the laboratory buried treated wood stakes in test plots from the Canadian border to the Mississippi Delta. Every few years they test and examine these stakes. The results reveal that treated wood, like the Energizer bunny, just keeps going and going and going. Both Venice, Italy, and the Brooklyn Bridge are perched on pilings made of wood. If it's good enough for these titans, it's good enough for little Oma Tupa.

In creating the crawl space, we've also created a potential catch basin for rain, runoff, and groundwater to accumulate. I cover the walls with a waterproof membrane. I surround the bottoms of the walls with drain tile that leads to a plastic sump bucket in the crawl space. Inside this sump bucket is a pump that will eject the water when it reaches a certain level. Without the pump the crawl space would become a small underground swimming pool. A muddy, cold, unwanted swimming pool. And during the second spring of the cabin's young life, the pump fails and we get our indoor pool.

VI

Kat

WIFE, LIFESAVER,
CARPENTER

When you marry, you marry the whole person —
not just the parts above the waterline.
You get both the silk sails and the barnacles.

K AT IS THE MOST ENERGETIC person on the planet. She has two speeds: full throttle and fast asleep. Born without dimmer switch or brake, she'll do two loads of wash, walk the dog, dash off a dozen e-mails, and clean the kitchen in the morning before I can muster the energy to grab the cup of coffee she's stealthily delivered to our bedside. She is the queen of multitasking. She is a woman who not only knows how to work hard but does. So it is not a far-fetched notion to imagine she'll continue that hummingbird pace with a tool belt on.

Building on a lake inclines one toward boat analogies. And it's like this: When you lash two boats together, you don't just join ropes, but sails and anchors as well. When you marry, you marry the whole person — not just the parts above the waterline; you get both the silk sails and the barnacles.

Kat and I were launched from two very different piers. Kat's father was sixty when she was born; mine was half that age. I was born at the start of the baby boom, Kat toward the end. Kat grew up in the rural town of Bemidji; I grew up in the white-collar suburbs of Minneapolis. Kat's father was a jack-of-all-trades who built a house single-handedly when he was seventy. My dad was a patent lawyer; his most ambitious home improvement project was changing the washer in our kitchen faucet, and that with mixed success. Kat's mom was wonderfully reclusive; mine, the extroverted owner of a small dress shop. When Kat was in her early twenties, she was a hard-driving Tupperware saleswoman; at that age I was a hard-partying hippie carpenter.

If you were to graph our lives and lifestyles, you would see them zigging and zagging in divergent directions, until they intersected in 1993. And while my graph lines began veering a bit more toward the calm and conservative, Kat's veered a little more toward the loose and liberal. Our lines and lives crisscrossed, on bicycles, on just the right day, at just the right speed, on a rain-slick rural road — enough serendipity to give a man religion.

We met on an MS 50 fund-raising bike ride amid a throng of three thousand. Kat was riding with her two daughters, Sarah and Kellie, and I with my son Zach. Halfway through the ride, it started raining. A few hundred riders massed under a canopy erected as a rest stop. Zach made some small talk with an outgoing woman with short hair. She and I exchanged pleasantries; waited for the rain to let up; then, at our own paces, headed out. We passed one another and parried and feinted for a few miles. Kat's daughters continue to maintain Kat was first attracted not to my personality but to my rear view. Eventually this woman and I fell into a comfortable, conversational speed.

Since our paths would never cross again — we lived forty miles from each other, on opposite ends of town — we told each other our life stories; the good, the bad, and the ugly. She was refreshingly honest; actually, refreshingly everything. By the time we pedaled under the arc of balloons at the finish line, I was plotting ways I could make our paths cross again. I'd been studying the literature and had ascertained that women of a certain age liked men with (1) hair, (2) a job, (3) therapy, and (4) at least a year of divorce under their belts. I was feeling in the high-percentile category.

I was over forty, with heavily oxidized dating skills. I'd dated way too soon after my divorce and in doing so had already thrown one relationship under the bus. In another misadventure I went on a blind date and, while having coffee, got hit in the head with a rock propelled from a lawn mower across the street. I went on another date with a woman who had a PhD in making men feel small. I should have taken a hint: my lot in life was to live a life of lonely celibacy — with a helmet on.

But I connived a way to see Kat again. It was still in the days of film and snail mail. I took a picture of Kat, Kellie, and Sarah, then wheedled out her address and phone number to send her copies; in this digital age of e-mail we might never have seen each other again.

The future walks a tightrope made of dental floss; good and bad things happen every day without rhyme or reason. A butterfingered tenant puts an air conditioner in his apartment window above the pet shop the moment you go in to buy a chew toy for Bobo. Or an angel in biking shorts — one who after a decade of up-and-down dating had decided she was perfectly happy without a man in her life — stops to get out of the rain at the exact same point in time that you do. A thousand things could have scuttled our meeting: a flat tire, a five-mile-per-hour-stronger wind, a wrong turn, a different pace.

The leap of faith Kat took in marrying me is the leap of faith by which all others are measured. It was Evel Knievel-esque. I wouldn't have married me if I were me. I'd been a single dad for over a year, and my housekeeping skills were all garnered from the *Jed Clampett Book of Etiquette*. I was the fun dad. On birthdays we'd decorate cakes with skyrockets and set them off — in the house. We had a Mexican hammock suspended in a large doorway off the living room. We had a basketball hoop mounted high on a kitchen wall where we'd play

H-O-R-S-E with a grapefruit-size basketball, calling shots like "bounce shot off the refrigerator door" and "hook shot over the light fixture."

It would be blasphemy to call my cooking skills "skill." Because I was a single dad, we were tight on money and did most of our shopping at Sam's Club. We'd buy forty-packs of Bagel Bites and jars of peanut butter that required two hands to lift. Most nights I'd get home at 5:30 and try to wedge in a meal before a soccer game or concert. Even today the bar is set dangerously low in terms of what my kids consider a "great dinner," since their point of reference is Wonder Bread with Velveeta melted over it.

Because of other factors above and beyond the presence of the basketball court in the kitchen, the house did look, maybe even smelled a bit, like a gymnasium. For the first eight months of our separation, Nanny (my ex) and I "bird nested." We each kept a separate apartment, then alternated living in the house every three or four days while the kids stayed put. With the divorce imminent and our kids' worlds in turmoil, it seemed the least they were owed was this stability. But because of this arrangement, no one cleaned, dusted, organized, or imposed much in the way of discipline. "The dog's been peeing on the carpet? Well, she (or he) can just deal with that when she's (he's) here." "Not my turn to mow the lawn," and so on.

And this is the house Kat and daughters inherit when we decide to get married. This is the place the seven of us will call home.

Friends, family, and therapists alike winced at the notion of Kat, Sarah, and Kellie moving into the house I'd occupied in a previous lifetime. Blending two families is hard enough without doing it in a house filled with apparitions from the past; so we did our best to make it ours. We remodeled the house with a vengeance. Out went the 20-foot vaulted ceiling over the living room and in went Kellie's and Sarah's bedrooms. We resurfaced everything we could: new carpet, new paint, new wallpaper, new sinks, new landscaping, new light fixtures, new contact paper. We scrubbed and purged.

At one point when tensions were high, we took the advice of a family counselor. "Native Americans would burn sage to purify old places," she explained. On the way home from that session, we stopped at a food co-op and bought a bundle of sage the size of a whiskbroom. We purified the house, room by room. This was no wimpy incense stick; this was a mobile bonfire. The smoke detector went off. We ground ash into the new carpet. But there isn't a bundle of sage large enough to make an old house 100 percent renewed. Oma Tupa, Oma Lupa will be 100 percent ours.

I'm a man with chronic bruises on his arms; the result of my pinching myself to make sure I'm awake. When I open my eyes in the morning and stretch south, I find this perfect thing in my arms. I hug a body that's sparse yet powerful. I gaze at a face I never tire of. I brush back a leaf of hair and, knowing that after she opens her eyes for a wink, I'll stare into brown eyes that radiate goodness. She's a woman tender by nature but confident by will. She's intelligent and street smart. She never flinched when checking her heart to see if there was room for three more kids — something I'll always honor her for. No one can make me laugh harder. No one can make me feel calmer. There's no one I trust more. She's my best friend. I'll die knowing I had at least one true thing in this world.

Kat and I transport nearly every stick of lumber down to the building site, and we transport our emotional baggage as well. But we don't transport much liquor-store booty. If you were to look at the scorecard that tracks our genetic disposition toward alcoholism, you'd find us both batting a thousand. We both grew up in households where alcohol was an "issue." Knowing this tweaked us, in different ways. Kat used this information to steer clear of trouble; I used it as an excuse to drive into it.

Kellie, Tessa, and Kat strike a pose with their
nail guns and finish sanders.

Kat opted for abstinence for twenty-five years. She drifted into moderate territory and eventually had her party days, but she kept hold of the reins.

I, on the other hand, began a twenty-year love affair with the Woodstock lifestyle from the moment I started college until I crashed and burned in my late thirties. I was the guy who ate the worm from the bottom of the mezcal bottle. I was the guy who wrote the term paper "The Therapeutic Uses of LSD" and used himself as the lab rat. So while the past is choppy, Kat and I have kept this part of our lives under control and aboveboard. She'll have an occasional drink but never overdoes it. I simply stopped playing with fire. When people ask why I don't drink, I tell them, "I got it all out of the way at an early age."

It takes Kat a while to get the hang of the hammer. After installing one beam, she drives home a 16d nail, leaving forty half-moon pecker marks from missed swings. I write "Kat did this" next to all the marks, telling her I didn't want my buddies coming up next weekend to think I'd missed that many swings. Kat thinks this is very un-funny. She tears up, feels hurt. I'm glad when the quip gets covered by drywall. And I'm glad to be married to a woman who'll give me a running start at an apology.

Eventually Kat begins to take pride in her carpentry skills. Her lingo and hammer-swinging abilities improve to where she has a bit of jauntiness to her. On her way to the cabin one weekend, Kat stops at Menards home center and asks where the women's work gloves are. The clerk directs her to the gardening gloves. That's a mistake. Kat tells him she wants *real* work gloves. "I have a tool belt," she informs the squirming kid.

And it is a momentous day when we drive the forty miles into Grand Marais to purchase Kat's first power tool — a random orbital sander. She's been sanding the exposed beams and the belt sander is damn near impossible to hold overhead. The hardware store has three models. She fondles each, test drives them one by one along the edge of the shelf as if it's running. She examines the paper securing detail – Velcro or self-stick. I watch her evaluate the tools. If possible, I fall a little bit more in love. The yellow DeWalt is cheerier-looking and lighter, but the Makita is twenty dollars cheaper. The Skil is thirty dollars cheaper, but it also feels thirty dollars cheaper. And what a ho-hum color. Kat always goes for quality. We walk out of Buck's Hardware with the DeWalt.

When it comes to hands-on work, we have similar habits. We both tear into a job, stay on task, and don't clean up until it's finished. I'd rather keep my momentum and trip over a logjam of 2×4 scraps all day long, than take 30 seconds to clean them up. When Kat insulates there are exploded bags of fiberglass everywhere. She cooks the same way; after a simple dinner of pasta, the kitchen looks like the cafeteria in *Animal House*. The difference is, when Kat's done she cleans up — fast, of course. I can leave a mess for days, weeks, months.

There are some old habits that die hard when it comes to building. When I had my own construction company, I always had gophers (go fer this, go fer that). That's what I was accustomed to — but not Kat. She didn't get the gopher thing. She'd ask me to get her nails (did I hear that right?). And when I needed something I often got "just a minute" (uppity apprentice!). I had to recalibrate. I had to remember this wasn't a construction company, it was a marriage.

We sometimes tackle jobs together, we sometimes work side by side on separate tasks. Either way we keep each other's spirits up. We remind each other about Rule # 1: "It's gotta be fun." When things get too un-fun we head for the deck overlooking the lake. We eat Doritos, smoke a cigarette, neck, take a catnap, take a hike — do something to break the un-fun cycle.

Yet we have our moments. Late in the project we decide to install cedar shingles in the triangular gable ends of the cabin. Kat spends the better part of a day priming and painting hundreds of cedar shingles. I tack up a few, and it just doesn't look right. I think it would look much better if we installed natural cedar shingles, ones with round tips like fish scales that create a cool-looking pattern. Kat gets fuming. It's times like this I wish God had given me the tongue physiology to link together the letters *S, O, R, R,* and *Y,* but it's just not there. Hell knoweth no fury like that of a woman who hath painted little friggin' shingles for three hours only to have their use rejected by a boneheaded husband.

There are other commandments I break during the building process, including:

- Thou shalt not use-eth thy wife's bread knife to cut Styrofoam insulation.
- Thou shalt not use thy wife's car to fetch gas for thy chain saw, especially if thy gas can hath a pinhole in it. For thy days will be long in the line at the car wash.
- Thou shalt not covet thy wife's favorite T-shirt, especially if, after it hath been coveted, thou use-eth it as a paint rag.
- Thou shalt not use the turkey baster to removeth old gas from thy Weed Wacker.
- Thou shalt not leave thy slowly leaking air compressor plugged in while thy wife stays alone at the cabin, for when it turn-eth on at two in the morning, it will scare the ever-loving shit-eth out of her.
- Thou shalt not forget thy wife's birthday and at the last minute buyeth her a bird feeder from Julie's Hardware Store.
- Thou shalt not forget to call thy wife after a day in which thou hast shingled much, for she will fear thou hast broken thy frigging neck.
- Thou shalt not maketh fun of thy wife's attempts to grout tile.
- Thou shalt not drink the last ginger ale when thy wife hath menstrual cramps.
- And most sinful of all: Thou shalt not use a utility knife to cut-eth out the last two pages of thy wife's Nicholas Sparks novel as a practical joke.

We all have character flaws that follow us around like toilet paper stuck to the heel of our shoe. Everyone but us can see it. Everyone knows where we've been, and it's tremendously funny, but it's a little embarrassing to point it out and it's not that big of a deal, so people just let it go. Everyone drags around a little Charmin. It's your coworker eyeing the new VP position. Everyone knows there's zero chance he will get the promotion, but he's grinning. He knows he's gonna get it. Toilet paper on the heel. It's your friend cooking the perfect dinner, and you know somewhere along the line, she'll misread the "three minutes" on the package as "thirty"; Charmin on the heel. One of the many trails of toilet paper stuck to the bottoms of Kat's and my shoes has the words "Doesn't know when to quit" written on it.

One day Kat is painting. She (1) lacks patience, (2) doesn't like painting, (3) is working much on a day we vowed to not work much. I can see it coming. "Put the paintbrush down, step away from the window, and no one will get hurt." But she's hell-bent on finishing. Then there are tears and enamel paint dripping everywhere. It's a bloody wreck. Later that night even Dick's rum and Coke and Jean's potatoes can't save the patient. Ain't that somethin'? On our wedding rings Kat and I inscribed, "Shared joy is double joy; shared sorrow is half sorrow." But the equation doesn't work all the time.

But we learn about paint and Charmin and each other and when to call it quits. And we learn one of the places we never call it quits is in taking the person for who they are. We learn that our role isn't to turn each other into the person we think they should be, but to help them become the best version of who they want to be. If my wedding ring were wide enough, I'd inscribe that, too.

Second marriages are different; they better be, because if not, you're looking at a third, fourth, and fifth. The grim fact is, two-thirds of all second marriages fail. By the time you say "I do" a second time, you better know that the person you're marrying is the person you're marrying — not someone you hope he or she will become. You better have learned to ride the compromise train.

Something got miswired in many marriages of my generation, the peace and love era. Simon and Garfunkel said I'm supposed to be kickin' down the cobblestones, feeling groovy, but during my first marriage I'm trudging down some dark alley feeling plenty pissed off about something. Long hair couldn't shroud the problems, love beads couldn't make up for the lack of communication. No cobblestones, not groovy. And you know what, lamppost? I don't give a rat's ass about "what ya' knowin'." I had to grow up before marrying Kat.

One weekend we drive fifty miles to Duluth to watch Grandma's Marathon — one of the ten races claiming the title "most scenic marathon in the country." We find a spot at mile twelve and plunk down. It's dumbfounding to watch the front-runners: a pack of twelve running a five-minute, five-second-per-mile pace. But it's those that come behind that hold a place in Kat's heart. The year we met, Kat was training for the Twin Cities Marathon. She'd joined the American Lung Association

Kat with her tool belt

Running Club (ALARC) — a group that prides itself on a ninety percent–plus finish rate — and followed the training regimen. For Kat this was more than a long run; it was a year-long workout for strengthening lungs, legs, and pluck.

Three weeks before the marathon, her right leg begins plaguing her. Nothing torn or broken, just a slow, dull, rising pain. She has dozens of supporters and a few doubters. Her boss bets her twenty dollars she doesn't finish — a guarantee she will finish. Neither of our mothers can grasp the concept of why anyone would run twenty-six miles when they could drive.

The day of the race we establish a game plan: The kids and I will meet her at the three-, ten-, fifteen-, and twenty-mile marks and at the finish. She has trained at a nine-minute-per-mile pace. But at mile marker three she doesn't come by at twenty-seven minutes — or thirty minutes — or thirty-five. She comes by at thirty-seven, with a bandanna wrapped around her right leg, limping, frustration in her eyes. Something has torn. A smart husband would have wrapped his arms around her right there and — kicking and screaming or not — carried her to the car. But she insists on continuing. She finishes but with an injury so severe it prevents her from running distances for two years. Kat can sympathize with the ones running at the rear.

Kat has a rare yet very endearing disease: Robin Hood Syndrome (RHS). She robs from the rich and gives to the poor, with us being the rich, though we're not, and the poor being just about anyone. Her philanthropy is spontaneous, carried out in guerrilla-like fashion, and based on "the look in her (or his or their) eyes."

It's like this. She's shopping at a department store and notices a young woman of clearly modest means, repeatedly taking a dress off a rack, holding it up to herself in the mirror, caressing the hem, then putting it back. Kat sees Cinderella with nothing to wear to the ball. She sees the longing "look in her eyes." Kat slides the sales clerk her credit card, buys the dress for Cinderella, then disappears incognito.

The kid in front of her at the gas station has a panicked "look in his eyes" as his credit card is rejected. A tankful of gas, an armload of food, and the kid's nerves sit in limbo. Kat tells the clerk to put everything on her card, and the kid is flabbergasted.

"Gee, thanks, lady," he says as he waits for the strings attached. Robin Hood attaches no strings.

She secretly pays the utility bill for the family of one of our kid's friends that's had their gas turned off. She buys coats, meals, groceries for the unexpecting, unassuming, and, probably at times, undeserving. She knows the "look in their eyes" well, because those eyes once stared back at her in the mirror. I hope they never develop an antidote for RHS.

Sometimes, when Kat and I see an older couple, we play the "I wonder if we'll be like that when we're old?" game. We see a couple in their eighties at the symphony. They shuffle with the same length of stride. They're the same height, as if sixty years of seeing eye to eye has recalibrated their skeletons. They both wear a sophisticated gray. They look alike. Decades of sharing saliva, sperm, and tears has intermingled their DNA. They look at each other and kiss. That's us, yes, surely that's us. End of game.

And we see a middle-aged couple at a Denny's. The few words exchanged are cold and edgy like cardinals flying hard into a picture window. There is no surprise in what's ordered. The silence does not appear to discomfort them. Nope. That's not us.

We meet Ken and Vi at the health club. "I'm Vi, and this is Ken. It's easy to remember, just remember Vi-Ken," the mnemonic based on Minnesota's football team. They're sixty-five-plus and at the club every afternoon. They always wear twin T-shirts emblazoned with a running or biking event they've completed together. Not wimpy ones either;

Ironman 100 bike ride, Grandma's Marathon, even MS 50 shirts. They lift weights and spot for each other. Some folks set their eyes on a condo in Arizona for their retirement prize. On the day Vi-Ken retired (both on the same day) they hopped on their tandem bike, pedaled 450 miles to Manitoba, then turned around and rode to the Gulf of Mexico. It took them two months. Uh-huh, that's us.

And as we get to know Dick and Jean, who sold us the land, we think, "That's us." They didn't bike 1,500 miles for retirement; Dick was too beaten up from years of working heavy construction. They bought a 28-foot motor home and drove south. Probably passed Vi-Ken on the way. We admire our neighbors-down-the-shore in every way. They clearly enjoy each other's company. After decades of marriage they've learned each other's rough spots and handle them like a good shock absorber. They're always welcoming, always willing to lend a hand. Dick usually has an Ole and Lena joke and wisdom to dispense while looking over the top of his reading glasses. I'm going to stop a few words short of saying Dick was a father figure to me — but it was close. They are good people. Uh-huh, that's us, too.

Ain't that somethin'.

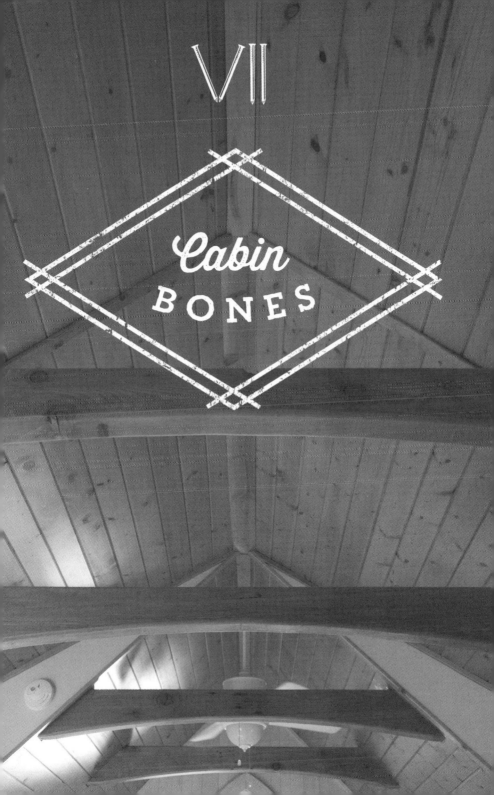

VII

Cabin BONES

Destiny can throw down a pretty sparse
trail of popcorn for you to follow.

SPRING SLINKS ITS WAY INTO northern Minnesota and finds there's
still nothing vertical rising from the cabin floor. It's not like we've
been cutting bait this whole time. Getting the driveway in, the electricity down the hill, and the floor framed have all been essential. But a
cabin needs walls and a roof.

I order lumber, head north, and start whacking together the first wall.
I've built the cabin so many times in my head that my only blueprint is a
smudged sheet of graph paper tucked in my back pocket. We've decided
to build the walls using 2×6s. This gives us a thicker cavity for insulation: 6-inch stuff with an R-value of 19, instead of the R-value of 13 you
get in 2×4 walls. Two by six construction will not only make the cabin
more energy efficient in the long run, but the walls will be heavier in
the short run.

Using the floor as a gigantic workbench, I build the 16-foot-long,
12-foot-high front wall. It contains a mammoth structural header to
support the wall and roof over the opening for the 9-foot patio door.
The header alone pushes 100 pounds. The conventional way to lift a
wall after it's built is to first toenail the bottom plate along a chalk line
snapped on the edge of the floor. You use a pry bar to slightly lift the
top of the wall so you can slip a few 2×4 blocks under it, providing space

for your fingers when you start lifting. You lay some long 2×4s in the vicinity so you can brace the ends of the wall, once it's raised. Then in a clean-and-jerk motion, you lift the wall from horizontal to a 45-degree angle to vertical in a motion resembling the raising of the flag at Iwo Jima. Normally you do this with a crew of three or four, but this element is something I sorely lack. No problem.

I get everything ready, then take a deep breath and go for the dead lift. When I was a twenty-five-year-old young buck carpenter in Denver, I built entire houses with just one other person. I lifted 30-foot-long walls and hauled trusses up two or three stories by brute force. It doesn't register that I'm a quarter of a century older until I start lifting the wall. I wrestle it up knee-high and stop. *Oof da* — wood's gotten heavier over the last couple decades, eh?

I let the wall slam back down. Clearly I need to depend on physics more than physique. I cut a pair of 3-foot-long 2×4s, grunt one corner of the wall high enough to prop the support under it, then go to the other end, lift and put the other support under that end. This I can barely handle, but the wall is moving in the right direction. I cut 5-foot-long 2×4s, repeat the same procedure, and the top of the wall swings upward another 2 feet. Better. Higher. The angle of the wall is getting to a point where the bottoms of the next pair of supports might kick out from under the rising wall. I cut a metal joist hanger in half and nail the halves, pointy end down, to 7-foot 2×4s and lift one corner again. The points dig into the subfloor so the support can't slide. This is working pretty slick. This is genius. I start lifting the other end so I can install the other support, and suddenly my world is spinning. The wall is twisting and falling. I dive out of the way, and the 500-pound wall spins and crashes to the floor. The header misses my head by inches. The nails holding the bottom plate have given way, creating a twisting, out-of-control wall. I am within inches of becoming construction roadkill. I assess the damage: torn pants, gashed knee, bruised ego, wall back flat on the floor but now teetering half off the deck, heart rate about 600.

The good part about working alone is there's no one to see your clumsiest moments. The bad part is if you really screw up, you can get yourself into serious trouble; even into the everafter. I dismantle the wall to make it half as heavy, then stand it in pieces. Lesson learned. I'm fifty-ish, out of shape, working alone. I get it.

The remaining 12- and 16-foot-tall walls I tackle with Goldwater-like conservatism. I build the walls in manageable sections and stand them sanely. Over the course of several days I get all the exterior walls stood and braced. I hand nail everything. I have air equipment I could use to speed things up, but the grind of the compressor, the pow-pow-pow of the nail gun, and the way hearing protection makes you feel like you're working inside a marshmallow seem out of place in Crystal Bay.

These walls, while not glamorous, are the skeleton. Every other component will be hung from, run through, stuffed into, or nailed to it. It receives no glory, no accolades, no soft strokes of admiration. When the last piece of drywall is hung, you won't even be able to tell this skeleton is there. But it's what makes a cabin, a cabin; so essential that when God started fiddling around with his second human being he didn't start with a heart, muscle, or brain. He started with a part of the skeleton: the rib.

In a standard house wall, the studs — as well as floor joists and roof rafters — are positioned every 16 or 24 inches; this pattern is usually disturbed only when punctuated by a window, door, or interior wall. The numbers *16* and *24* in the world of construction are, if not magical, efficient: Four studs spaced at 16 inches or three studs spaced at 24 inches create the perfect home for standard 48-by-96-inch sheets of plywood, drywall, oriented strand board, sheet siding, and other paneling. Batts of insulation are designed to fit snugly in these 16- and 24-inch spaces. Most other building materials — siding, moldings, trim, hardwood flooring, carpet, and vinyl flooring — come in 8-, 12- and 16-foot lengths so they too can take advantage of these efficiencies. Even many tools — tape measures (with their tick marks at 16-inch intervals), drywall squares (with their 4-foot-long arms), framing squares (with their 16- and 24-inch legs) — are designed around these golden numbers. There is a rhythm, a pattern, a logical economy. But this cabin is so cut up by pockets for floor beams and openings for windows, the pattern is hard to detect. It's a lot of head scratching and oddball spacing, and while I'm not able to take full advantage of standardized measurements, I'm glad to have them.

If you go back far enough you'll discover standard measurements weren't developed by a task force, but over time. The original "inch" was based on the width of a person's thumb (or, if you were King Edward in 1324, the length of "three barley corns, round and dry"), the "foot" was based on (no great surprise) the length of a man's foot, and the "yard" was based on the distance between the tip of the middle finger on an outstretched arm and the tip of the nose. While it was impossible to misplace these measuring devices, discrepancies in lengths were a given. I would guess if you wanted your money's worth back then when building you would hire tall carpenters with large feet and thumbs.

Most new houses today are "platform framed," meaning you build in layers. You build a floor, raise a set of 8-foot walls on top of that, build another floor (or roof) and keep heading upward. Every component, whether it's a 2×4 or a sheet of plywood, is easily carried by a single person. You always have a platform to work from, and things are rarely more than 2 feet above your head.

Walls in older homes, as well as in our cabin, are "balloon framed," where the studs stretch continuously from bottom to top, from foundation to roof. Floors in between are "hung from" the walls. The term "balloon frame" originated in the mid-1800s when the transition was being made from building houses from logs and hefty timbers to building them with 2×4s sheathed with boards. Skeptical carpenters thought the new method so flimsy that houses framed this way would blow away — like a balloon.

We balloon-frame the cabin, not for nostalgia but for strength. The floor that links the tall sides of the cabin together will prevent the weight of the roof — in a perpetual state of trying to do the splits — from forcing the second-floor knee walls outward.

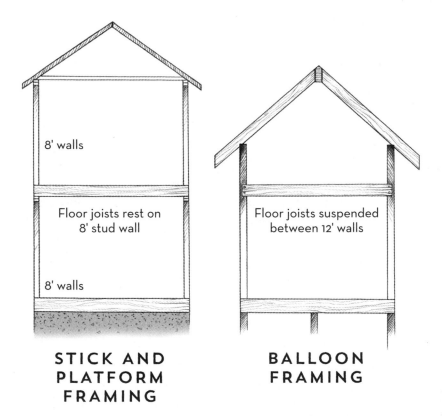

8' walls

Floor joists rest on
8' stud wall

8' walls

Floor joists suspended
between 12' walls

STICK AND PLATFORM FRAMING

BALLOON FRAMING

Kat comes up for a long weekend. After six years my heart still bungee jumps when I see her low-gearing it down the driveway. One of our missions is to heft the 200-pound salvaged floor beams in place. Again, what Kat lacks in arm strength she makes up for in fortitude. She insists on carrying and installing her half of the beam. I watch her with her tool belt on, hoisting beams, straining, pounding nails in whack after whack, converting to the two-handed swing when she's exhausted. I see nothing but strength. *Sisu*, the Finns call it.

Kat is constantly pushing for more windows. I think the cabin, with a 9-foot patio door, 5-foot picture window, two skylights, and a dozen other windows is already approaching greenhouse status. Kat keeps trying to picture the views. "I want to see the lake when I'm chopping carrots." "Wouldn't it be nice to see cars when they drive down the driveway?" "I'd *love* to see that big pine when I'm sitting on the couch." She wants another kitchen window, which will open the view but in our small kitchen will eliminate the option of even one upper cabinet. For Kat, me, and Oma Tupa, it's hunt, peck, and compromise. And we always find, if we talk long enough, if we listen long enough, if we think long enough, we find a solution we can both live with. We find a way to make an extra window fit — we'll figure out where the dishes go later.

And herein lies both the danger and beauty of building with only a smudged piece of graph paper in your back pocket. With an eighteen-page, architecturally drawn blueprint — (the road map for building most houses) — changes are difficult to coordinate. If something changes here, it changes something else over there. Midstream alterations become expensive; too many can slow the project down and throw off the schedule. The contractors, scheduled to finish the project like a well-choreographed dance troupe, begin to step on one another's toes. But with a graph paper print and no client, every window, nail, and board is subject to debate.

Kat and I work long days until our arms, our patience, and the daylight fail us. The romantic, made-for-TV version of the end-of-the-day has us cooking chili over a campfire, chatting as the moon rises, then crawling into a tent overlooking the lake, rocked to sleep by the rhythm of the waves. But the real life end-of-the-day version is this: We're bone tired, dirty, clammy, and stinky. Mostly we've eaten little triangular egg salad sandwiches encased in plastic from a nearby gas station. The softest thing we've sat on is a plastic resin chair.

So many nights we drive the seven miles to the Mariner Motel and collapse. The proprietor is grouchy at first. He's fed up with cable installers and taconite workers tracking god-knows-what all over his carpets. His guests steal alarm clocks, wipe oily hands on bath towels, leave tables full of beer cans. Three novas short of a four-star rating, the place doesn't draw a sterling clientele. But eventually he warms up; even talks a little fishing. And in Room 17 we revel in the orgasmic touch of a warm shower, the luxurious feel of clean sheets, and the mindless diversion of *MASH* reruns. Exciting? No. Sustaining? Yes.

For the last few summers I've gone to the Boundary Waters Canoe Area Wilderness (BWCAW) with three friends. This summer I beg off, needing the time to build. But Travis, Bruce, and Dave make an irresistible offer: the three will come work for a couple of days; then, with a week's worth of work done in two days, I can go canoeing guilt-free. I will stay on schedule, though there is no schedule.

Their projected arrival coincides with framing the roof. Perfect. Installing the rafters and plywood is a team endeavor, but figuring out the angle and cut of the rafters is a solo activity, so I tackle this before they arrive.

Most roofs today are built using trusses. They look light and flimsy, but through the marvel of triangulation, the 2×4 and 2×6 members create a surprisingly robust roof. Truss manufacturing has literally become a science. You punch into a computer the distance the trusses need to span, the weight or load they need to carry, the pitch of the roof and other factors, and the program spits out the length and angle of every little piece that goes into the truss. The program relays this information to "smart saws" that efficiently cut the components and to "smart assembly tables," where the pieces are arranged, then joined with metal plates hydraulically pressed into the wood.

The same little pieces of wood that zigzag through each truss to give them their strength are also the source of their greatest weakness: the space within them is largely unusable. We need to take full advantage of the living space below our roof, so we opt to hand-frame the roof using 2×12s to create a vaulted ceiling. These 2×12s provide both strength and a deep cavity for installing thick batts of insulation later on.

I use the floor as a life-size piece of graph paper, using chalk lines to indicate the position and thickness of the exterior walls. I place one end of a 2×12 rafter-to-be on this imaginary wall, use a little geometry to determine the 45-degree pitch, and draw in the ridge board where the rafters will meet at the peak. I check and recheck, then mark the cut lines on the 2×12. This will become my pattern for marking the rest of the rafters; they'll all be the same, either all right or all wrong. I use a circular saw to cut the angle at the peak where it will meet the ridge board and the triangular-shaped "birdsmouth" where it will rest on the walls. I trace around paint cans to create the wing-shaped rafter tails that will become the eaves and use a jigsaw for cutting those. I use the same method to figure out the rafters for the dormers, which are a different pitch, to create even more headroom in the loft. Then I mark out and cut rafters until darkness falls.

Travis, Dave, and Bruce arrive at the cabin, and the "many hands make light work" proverb turns true. Travis and Dave, nail guns in hand, bang up a clearly non-OSHA-approved scaffold made of 2×4s along one side of the cabin. By nightfall all the upper walls are sheathed and braced and most of the rafters are cut.

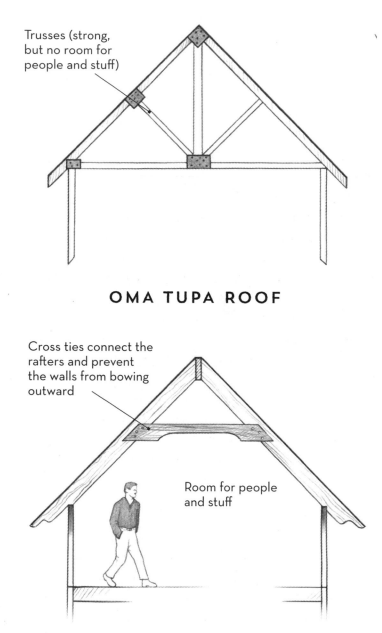

ORDINARY ROOF

Trusses (strong, but no room for people and stuff)

OMA TUPA ROOF

Cross ties connect the rafters and prevent the walls from bowing outward

Room for people and stuff

The next day we start in earnest on the roof. We perform high aerial feats to install the ridge board to support the tops of the rafters. Bruce, sort of the Don Rickles of cabinetmakers, fires broadsides at us while continuing to cut the rafters on solid ground. We install the rafters, one of us securing them at the peak, the other two nailing them to the outer walls. My calculations are right, and the rafters fit tight and true. To sheathe the rafters we carry, swing, push, and grunt the plywood, bucket-brigade style, from driveway to roof. We are frigging machines. We may be slightly rusted frigging machines, but we're still machines. By the end of the second day, Oma Tupa, Oma Lupa has its hat on. And it's hats off to Bruce, Dave, and Travis.

In the late afternoon of the second day, Bruce hollers from a spot below the cabin where he's relieving himself, "Bring a level down here. Something looks waaaay strange down here."

My first instinct is to blow him off, since Bruce is a woodworker and might consider anything $1/16$th of an inch out of plumb "waaaay strange." I bring the 4-foot level down to discover that one of the nine vertical support posts he is looking at is indeed waaay strange. About 5-inches-out-of-plumb strange. Gulp.

Travis and Dave come down and are similarly appalled. One or 2 inches out of plumb   well, that you can chalk up to moderate negligence. But a post this perilously out of plumb is a felony. Worse yet, the other posts aligned with it are equally out of whack, but being shorter are not as noticeable. In my haste to build the floor and build upward, I've neglected to install cross bracing to keep the posts straight and plumb. This isn't just an aesthetic problem; it's a structural dilemma.

Carpenters love riddles, but this has no easy solution. The bottoms of the posts can't be moved because (a) they're buried 4 feet underground, and (b) even if we could move them, they'd no longer sit on the concrete footing pads. The tops can't be moved because they support the corners of the floor where the weight-bearing walls sit and intersect. We halfheartedly try using a winch to rack the whole works

The crew, hard at work

back into place. Nada. We nail in belated cross braces and 2×4s to connect the leaning posts to the more solidly anchored crawl space walls. Dumb, dumb, dumb. If I'd spent ten minutes doing this initially, there would be no problem. Dumb, dumb, dumb. Like a tongue to a chipped tooth, I spend my hours of solitude on the canoe trip worrying about the damn posts.

Upon our return I pay the price for my haste. I toil for three days — stooped over, heart a-poundin' — to dig three more holes by hand, pour cement, and install additional posts to support the posts with vertigo.

To finish framing the walls and roof of the bump-out, I enlist the services of my old Denver carpentry partner and friend, John, who lives fifty miles north. We go back thirty years. In college we consumed ungodly quantities of Boone's Farm Apple Wine while trying to decipher the heady writings of James Joyce and John Lilly. Prompted by an experiment in Lilly's *The Center of the Cyclone,* we rounded up four friends one winter evening, joined hands while encircling an elm tree in the city park, and attempted to create a "resonating group circuit" to receive interplanetary messages. What we got was cold.

John was lured to northern Minnesota years ago after forming a friendship with an old-timer named Russ who'd help build the Gunflint Trail. He bought land from Russ — forty acres on Extortion Lake — with the only access via half a mile of bushwhacking or a full mile of canoeing. John built an 8-by-8-foot starter cabin, a 16-by-16-foot final cabin, and an outhouse using the skeletal remains of a moose as the main structure. There was no electricity or telephone, and he fetched his water in five-gallon buckets from the lake. When John married, the

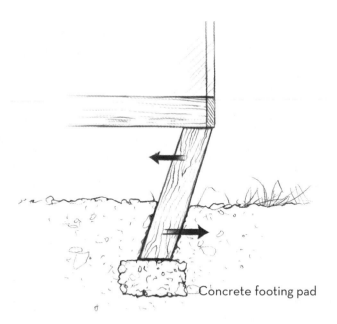

Concrete footing pad

LEANING POST DILEMMA

ceremony took place on a cliff overlooking the lake, the justice of the peace paddling in by canoe. John lives in town now but hangs on to his wilderness retreat.

It was John who showed me the door to carpentry. The chain of events that put a hammer in my hand shows what a sparse trail of popcorn destiny can throw down for you to follow. I met John at Gustavus Adolphus (nickname: God-save-us, All-of us) College, a small-town liberal arts college with the emphasis on "small." The winters were long. To break the monotony of studying for finals, we'd swipe trays from the cafeteria, wax them up with margarine, then attempt to gain enough downhill momentum to hit the snowbank by the tennis court and cross the street on the fly. But mostly it was quiet.

I selected philosophy as a major, and when my father suggested I consider a degree in a field where there were more than three job openings in the world, I selected English lit. When he pulled me aside a second time, I upped the ante to English teacher. When I couldn't pass the foreign language requirement I defaulted to elementary education; I was a kid once, I knew how that whole thing worked. Upon graduating I landed a job at the Woods Free School in Denver — an alternative school where kids could do whatever they wanted and a third of the parents adhered to the then-popular psychology of primal screaming. After my second year of teaching I went looking for a summer gig.

About the same time John was hitchhiking to Denver for a visit and was picked up by a Vermonter, heading west to hook up with a friend of a friend, who was building houses. John wound up working with them as a laborer, and shortly after, I joined up with them, too.

When I started I knew nothing about carpentry. I didn't know walls were built flat, then raised into position. I didn't know how to change a saw blade. And I surely didn't realize how physically demanding the job would be. For the first week I couldn't open my right hand in the morning, it was so knotted up from swinging a twenty-eight-ounce hammer. And my left hand was clublike from whacking it with a twenty-eight-ounce hammer. My knees felt like they'd been transplanted from a camel. But by the end of the summer I had my own framing crew. I was making twice as much money and facing half as much stress (and screaming) as I did as a teacher, so I stuck with carpentry. In short, I did what all good hippies did in the seventies: went to college, got a degree, then became a carpenter.

John returned to Denver, and we became a two-man framing crew. We became so in synch, we could frame a house in three days. On days when we were in the flow we could make fifteen dollars an hour and had life by the gonads. We worked outside and were lean, tan, and, though the word probably hadn't been coined back then, ripped. We were our own bosses. We could wear what we wanted and work as much as we wanted. On lunch breaks we could smoke, eat Twinkies, and exchange tales of bizarre construction accidents — and chances were good the concrete crew working next door would swing over and do the same. The Jimmy Jingle girl who pulled up to the job site at noon peddling sandwiches, Coke, and Marlboros wore a bikini top and was bad at making change. We could sneer at those cruising to office jobs along I-25, imagining they were staring back at us in jealous longing. We were modern-day cowboys who rode into town in a '56 Dodge Power Wagon, slinging our hammers. We swaggered. If we cut ourselves we pinched the wound tight with duct tape and kept working. Hearing, eye, and fall protection were for wimps. Life was grand, and we've both hovered around the carpentry life since then.

———

John and I complete the small loft above the entryway, then hand-cut and install the rafters. We sheathe the roof with plywood and get the tar paper down. Things go like clockwork. Our rhythm, unspoken language, and carpentry ESP, established years ago, remain.

Kat and I decide to build the stairway now, though there's a risk the exposed fir stringers will get beat up while we build the rest of the cabin. But it's better the stringers than the knees. Carpentry is a young person's sport. It builds you up physically for the first few years, then starts tearing you down.

The first few steps of the stairway are triangular and fan like cards in a bridge hand, then launch into a straight shot to the loft. Stairways are part math, part sawdust. Each rise, or the height of each step, should be 8¼ inches or less. The run or width should be 9 inches or more. Rule of thumb says, combined, the rise and run should be between 17 and 19 inches; it's what the human stride comfortably handles. The heights of the steps should be within ¼ inch of each other or the rhythm that feet develop while ascending or descending gets broken. Space is at a premium, so we cheat a little on the math.

The interior framing goes quickly because there are only three walls: two to create the bathroom and one to create the entryway closet. That's it. Everything else is wide open.

———————

The rough shell of the cabin is complete. Kat and I stand back on the driveway. We finally get a feel for how it fits with the land and our fantasies. We note that the staggered roofs make it look like a plywood seagull flapping its wings. It has a snug yet open feel; when we look through the arched window in the back, we can see Lake Superior through the arched window in the front.

From the kitchen, bathroom, and loft windows, we're able to frame the views of the lake and woods. We lie on the second floor where our bed will be and realize we're high enough to see the splash from the thumper hole. Things that even the best blueprint can't show — the vibe, the texture, the sense of wonder — become tangible. We love what we've created nail by nail, compromise by compromise, blister by blister.

VIII

The
DRIVE

> If all the difficulties were known at the outset of a long
> journey, most of us would never start out at all.
>
> *– Dan Rather*

TWO HUNDRED TWELVE point seven miles from house door to cabin door. Three hours and fifteen minutes at sixty-five miles per hour, assuming a full tank of gas, a strong bladder, and no '76 Winnebagos in need of a valve job in front of you. But that 195-minute trip is mere theory. We've never done it. Maybe no one ever has. There are just too many things to do and see and eat and smell and touch and reminisce about between the Twin Cities and Oma Tupa.

———

Our urban base is St. Paul, one of the few cities on earth where you can hit a deer while committing a drive-by shooting. On Friday afternoons the exodus begins, traffic on I-35 North thick as smoke from a Marlboro straight. Boats in tow and pop-up campers make each vehicle twice as long, and the wheezing interstate can hold only half as much. You think the lungs of the North Shore can't hold it all; it will choke, gasp, die of cancer. A tumor irritated by all the foreign matter entering.

But twenty miles north of town the congestion loosens. The exhaled smoke begins to dissipate here and there. A small puff drifts off to western Wisconsin, a wisp or two into Hinckley, Duluth, and Cloquet. A few smoke rings waft lazily into the Boundary Waters Canoe Area and the Quetico. More settles into the hundreds of Ma-and-Pa Northwoods resorts. By the time you reach Silver Bay there's just a trace of smoke.

And you take a deep breath, forget about the emphysema of the big city, the yellow teeth of work, the long ash of stress.

━━━━

For Kat and me the drive is not only a getting-to but also an escaping from. It is a time to reprogram. The Dodge Dakota is our decompression bell, and we are deep-sea divers needing transition time to avoid the bends. It's a time spent purging worries about work and kids and home.

Kat has the strongest need to vent, and she does with abandon, sometimes talking work until we pass the Forest Lake exit, twenty miles up the road; on a bad week, North Branch. She'll spout off stories of deals gone bad and gone good. She bounces ideas off me. If it's a Friday she may wheel and deal via cell phone as we wend our way north. Sometimes I go silent; can't we leave work on the desk? For me discussing work just stirs things up. I need to let the sediment settle. But silence is unfair; we both grew up in households where silence could mean lots of things — and spent a lot of energy trying to figure it out and how to fix it. So I listen, talk, focus, because I know if she has a chance to drain down, she'll be all in, renewed and fresh when we reach the cabin.

Though a single leg of the journey can take four or five hours, there have been times we've done a complete home-to-cabin-to-home circuit in twenty-four hours; nine hours driving, eight hours sleeping just to spend seven productive — or sometimes seven not-so-productive — hours at the cabin. But the seven hours are not the point; the entire twenty-four-hour journey is what's important. The hours of driving, side by side, 15 inches from each other, forces Kat and me to connect. The "quality time" argument just doesn't cut it; it's a phrase concocted by busy parents and workaholic spouses to diminish the guilt of working too long and too hard. People need to marinate themselves in one another's presence for a genuine length of time. They need to breathe the same air.

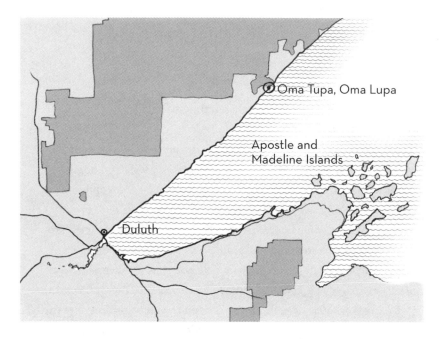

Oma Tupa, Oma Lupa

Apostle and
Madeline Islands

Duluth

And just as driving is a real part of the twenty-four-hour experience, sleeping is, too. Sleep is more than shut eyes. While we're building, sleep is blowing up the air mattress at 10:00 p.m., then blowing it up again, every hour on the hour. Sleep is reading by the glow of a construction clamp light. Sleep is being lulled by the water crashing in and out of the thumper hole below, a hollow in the rocky shoreline carved by millions of waves, grinding away one grain of sand per punch to create a 10,000-year-old percussion instrument. Sleep is waking in the darkness, feeling your way down sawdust-strewn stairs, stepping outside to pee and being met by a million stars or the lights of an ore freighter sliding by or the spilled-milk glow of the moon over Superior. Sleep is holding each other tight with drywall mud caked on tired hands. Sleep is feeling the vibrations from the Monson logging trucks barreling down Highway 61. Sleep is a slow waking to the realization you're at the cabin, not at home.

The twenty-four-hour journey is like the proverbial pig in the butcher shop where every part is used except the oink. Every part has a purpose. Every part counts. Every part is as real as the next. We remember to make the drive fun (Rule #1), and we do it without the hurry and scurry (Rule #2).

The joy-of-getting-there is not new. Even as a child, driving to my grandparents' cabin, The Roost, was as much fun as being there. Though the drive was only two hours, in my small-scale world it seemed as though we were journeying to Argentina. The night before departure, my sisters and I would turn the back of our Chevy Bel Air station wagon into first-class accommodations. We'd pack the back with pillows, blankets, Tootsie Rolls, Archie and Jughead comic books, the Cootie game, and crossword puzzle books. Once on the road we'd stick our heads out the windows to cool down, endlessly check the aerodynamics of our zigzagging hands. We'd bounce freely between front and back seats. In today's world my parents would serve hard time for child endangerment.

Singing was a major activity, and the Carlsen Chorale would belt out round after round of "When Sammy Put the Paper on the Wall," "We Are Climbing Jacob's Ladder," "Swing Low, Sweet Chariot," and "I Ain't a-Gonna Grieve My Lord No More." Looking back, it seems odd that the whitest family on the planet would sing so many black spirituals.

We played on-the-road games. Most popular was License Plate Bingo, in which I'd infuriate my sisters by claiming to have seen Hawaii. Or there was the memorization game "I'm going on a trip . . ." and the guessing game "Twenty Questions" and all ninety-nine verses of "Ninety-Nine Bottles of Beer on the Wall." No wonder the first question my grandfather asked my parents upon arrival was "stirred or shaken?"

There were some truly irresistible roadside attractions in the politically incorrect days of the sixties. There was an Indian reservation along Highway 169 where you could stop to buy chicken feather head-dresses, rubber tomahawks, and plastic tom-toms. For twenty-five cents you could SIT IN A TEEPEE WITH A REAL INDIAN.

There was an animal park where you could buy soda from a vending machine, pour it into the bowl of a caged black bear in the parking lot, then watch him slurp it up. There was a goat that chewed Dubble Bubble gum while standing on a tractor. "PETA-schmeta" was the attitude.

But some things never change. If you don't consider the "getting there" part of the vacation, you miss out on half of it.

———

Something happens when people gravitate toward vacationland. You can see it happen. That cold, straight, cast-in-place urbanism cracks. For some it grows into something soft and romantic; for others, wild and intense. But a vacation changes them. Those who thrive on 6:00 a.m. meetings, Brooks Brothers suits, and Tums trade it all in for blue jeans and a stack of midmorning pancakes. The lake dissolves the hard, tangled things at their core.

And the reverse is true, too. As they leave the big water, mile by mile, dashed line by dashed line, they sense a turning back into what they were. The softness hardens. The thing that guided them to the worn Adirondack chair to do nothing but daydream is pushing them toward a Steelcase desk and a Day-Timer. But like an agate, polished by years of back-and-forth tumbling, little by little they take on a permanent shine.

———

Often we have a kid or two or three along, which changes the dynamics. With two people there's one relationship (A+B); with three people there are four (A+B, B+C, A+C, and A+B+C); and with four people there are rapidly escalating eleven relationships (A+B, A+C, A+D, B+C, B+D, C+D, A+B+C, A+B+D, B+C+D, A+C+D, and A+B+C+D). With seven people — the population of our family — the number of combinations leaps exponentially.

And each of those combinations and relationships has its own history, rules, and boundaries. At first blush this seems like a mathematical exercise, but it's really an exercise in family dynamics. Whether it's a one-on-one conversation in the hallway or a full forum around the dinner table, the topics and depth get tweaked, bumped, and filtered according to peoples' sensitivities and the equation at hand. Our mathematically complex family is always working on the numbers.

No two trips are the same. Sometimes we only make it to the end of the driveway before returning to pick up some forgotten item — flour, drywall corner bead, Kat's headache medicine. Katie — our half-deaf, three-quarters-blind Pekingese — usually paces in the backseat until we've been on the road long enough for her to figure out we're not going to the vet's but to the cabin.

Usually the first stop is the town of Hinckley, where Tobie's — "Home of the World's Best Caramel Roll" — is located, and I think they're right. Glistening in goo and sugar, the size of a softball, they call like the Sirens to Ulysses. They're so sticky, the ladies at the cash register throw a moistened towelette in the bag for every roll. On a summer weekend northbound tourists stand six deep in front of the bakery counter with that same look of anticipation they had thirty years ago waiting to get into a Grateful Dead concert.

Location is everything, and Tobie's has location. Stationed halfway between Duluth and the Twin Cities, Tobie's is ideally positioned a bladder's capacity away from both. Started in 1920 as a café and bus stop, it was officially christened Tobie's in 1947 when Mr. and Mrs. Tobie Lackner purchased the place. Within a few years they were pumping over 300 dozen donuts, 1,000 rolls, and 60 pies a day into the gullets of northbound fishermen, truckers, and locals. It thrived on one premise: bake it gooey, and they will come. Tobie's was sold again in the mid-sixties, and the second and third generations of the Schrade family have inflated that one simple, megacaloric product into a mini-Disneyland. Around the perimeter of the parking lot sit an antique store, a gift shop, a gas station, a hotel, an ice cream parlor, and a now-defunct petting zoo; perhaps caramel-caked hands and shedding goat hair did not a good combination make.

Tobie's was dealt a royal flush when the Ojibwe tribe built the Grand Casino Hinckley two miles down the road. Relegated to reservations on Lake Mille Lacs and other areas in the 1800s, the Ojibwe now get their payback one quarter at a time. The synergies between Tobie's and the casino couldn't be better. Both draw twenty-four-hour-a-day people looking for a little something to do within radar range of the big city; people looking for the rush of a quick hit, whether it's jingling silver dollars or a sugar and caffeine buzz.

The two establishments are intertwined by the steady flow of big winners and big losers. At Tobie's you can surmise the degree of people's luck by the angle of their heads:

- Head held high: "Just call me Doc Holliday."
- Head pointed straight ahead: "Oooh, I wish I could do *that* over again."
- Head hanging low, hands rubbing back of neck: "What's Jimmy gonna say when he finds out the money for the bass boat is in the slot machine?"

Hinckley's other claim to fame is the Hinckley Fire of 1894. A desperately dry summer coupled with mountains of slash left by loggers created the perfect invitation for an inferno. On September 1 it knocked. The fire was so hot, houses burst into flames before the fire reached town. The emberlike glow of the firestorm could be seen in Iowa. Two hundred citizens clambered onto the Number 4 Limited train as it belched through town, pursued by flames. Those who survived submerged themselves in the shallow muck of Skunk Lake outside of town until the fire passed. Four hundred and thirteen residents were not as lucky.

The billboard outside the Hinckley Fire Museum depicting the disaster is not of the classic bright, blazing forest, but of smoky blackness tracking down a horrified woman. Inside are dishes welded together by the 1,500-degree heat, photos of the aftermath, and a life-size figure of Thomas Dunn hammering out his last telegraph message, "I think I've stayed too long."

———

When I see the Barnum exit, forty miles farther into the journey, deep memories get unbolted. It's here where two of my closest friends, Peter and Betsy, bought a farm right out of college. While many in the seventies read *Mother Earth News* and talked about a simpler, self-sufficient life, Peter and Betsy did it. They bought forty acres, heated with wood, concocted a homegrown hot sauce that made you see God, put up cords of zucchini, and lived close to the bone.

At their farm we'd set up our guitars and amps under the stars and jam until 3:00 a.m., the only neighbors to disturb having four feet or wings. On hungover mornings we'd listen to Dan Hicks & His Hot Licks while frying up huge batches of "everything eggs" — scrambled eggs containing everything identifiable from the refrigerator. On one of our bidaily runs to the Moose Lake Muni Liquor store, the spare tire in the trunk of Peter's '58 Chevy blew, and we thought we'd been hit by a meteorite until the dust cleared.

They sold the farm. Peter, Betsy, Nanny (my ex), and I bought some parcels of land deep in the Ozarks. Peter and Betsy were primed for the rugged lifestyle; they knew how to live simply from their years on the farm. They cut and peeled mountains of oak to build a cordwood home, started a garden, and got grooved out. We, though, found nothing simple in living simply. I spent hours every day hauling water from a nearby stream to a holding tank in the loft of a simple cabin we'd built. There were days all we could muster was to sit in front of a small RV fan run off a length of Romex wire connected to my truck battery. It all looked better in the pages of *Mother Earth News* than it did sitting in the 90-degree heat, 90 percent humidity of Gainesville, Missouri.

We struggled through four months of self-sufficiency; then within a two-week period, Maggie was born and my father died. We hit the back-to-the-land wall, retreated to the big city. Peter and Betsy moved closer to Kansas City and continued to lead a simple life for twenty more years. They pumped their water from a stream, grew their own food, delivered their two sons at home. Peter was a human Swiss Army knife who could fix or build anything. They were a couple that looked rock solid, but there were fissures. Peter hit a downward spiral and couldn't find the rewind button.

We lived our lives on parallel tracks; we both derailed. I was able to emerge from the wreckage with only broken bones and a broken marriage. Peter died of hepatitis C. So every once in a while, when I'm driving north and feel squishy inside, I'll take the side roads that lead to Peter and Betsy's old Minnesota farmstead. I'll slide the truck into park, squint my eyes, imagine Peter strumming his Gibson ES-335 singing "Ain't Nobody's Business" in the distance, and listen close.

To acclimate to North Shore time, Kat and I usually stop at Kitchi Gammi Park, also known as Pebble Beach, as we wind past Duluth. The nickname comes from the millions of Formica-smooth stones the waves have washed up and polished over the centuries. If there's even a trace of childhood left in you, you're skipping stones within minutes. In my toy mind I imagine stones saying, "Whoaaa, it took me 400 years to make it to shore; you're not going to ski-i-p-me-now-ow-ow?"

It's here you can first take in the contrasts that make Superior superior. You look right and see ore docks and mile-long coal trains, then left and see impossible rock formations. There's contrast in the people, too. Teenagers do fearless "I'm-going-to-live-forever" dives, fishermen fish, drunks drink, lovers love, kayakers kayak, and everyone snaps pictures.

Once while driving in we spot a small group of people surrounding a girl in a prom dress and her not-so-well-dressed date. We stop to use the Porta Potty, and a pastor — still working on his zipper — strides out. He takes a glance at us and invites us to the wedding. We turn and notice the girl in the prom dress is the bride. She's got a bun in the oven, and it's not from Tobie's. The congregation consists of nine people. The reception laid out on the picnic table is a Dairy Queen cake and a case of beer. Kat and I sit off to the side but listen and repeat the vows to each other like we're the ones getting married. The ten-minute ceremony is simple, honest.

Kat whispers, "Let's stick those twenties we just got from the cash machine into an envelope, give it to them, and git."

I maneuver the truck into getaway position. Kat dashes over, stuffs the envelope into the bride's hand, then runs away, yelling, "Thanks for helping us remember what love is all about." And we're outa there like bank robbers, checking the rear view mirror as the befuddled newlyweds stare.

But usually the trip goes like this: You burn hard through the first 100 miles of freeway (except for Tobie's) because it's mostly sod fields, outlet malls, and KFCs, then ease off the pedal at the rest stop overlooking Duluth and the harbor to stretch your legs and let your ears pop because of the elevation change. And it's hard to pass the Lake Street exit without hitting Father Time Antiques, fondling the cedar strip canoes in the Duluth Pack store, and grabbing a cup of java at the Blue Note. And if you hear the lift bridge horn, you are pulled like a snagged bass to the canal to watch the 700-, 800-, 1,000-foot taconite, grain, coal freighters pass through the canal. Then on to the Glensheen mansion, home of grandeur and homicide, where the tour guide won't let you even whisper about the room where Roger Caldwell took a pillow to his mother-in-law's face and a brass candlestick to the night nurse's head while drunk, henpecked, and in quest of inheritance.

And the hardest decision is whether to take the four-lane expressway, which gets you to Two Harbors in four John Hiatt songs or the ten-song Scenic Drive route, which clings to the shoreline and dips and weaves past ancient resorts that almost died and are now back in style because they're so out of style. And if you get caught behind a trailer-toting Duster driven by an old man new to the North Shore, it'll prolong your trip by half an hour, but it doesn't matter because you cross the Lester, French, and Knife Rivers, where smelt run and fishermen bob in inner tubes with molded legs, where the streams enter sometimes gently like ribbon and other times crash hard and angry like punches on a has-been boxer. And you see tourists on the side of the road putting the darnedest things in their trunks — birch branches and jagged rocks seem to be Mother Earth's best sellers. And past signs that say **NO STOPPING, NO SMELTING, NO TRESPASSING, NO DUMP-ING HOUSEHOLD TRASH, NO PASSING ON THE SHOULDER, NO OVERNIGHT PARKING**, but tourists say **YES** to them all.

Past Tom's Logging Camp, Mel's Smoked Fish, the Playing With Yarn store, Bob's Cabins, all things you miss if you take the four-lane highway a mile to your left, a highway so boring they put corrugated wake-up bumps on the shoulders. And the tradition is to stop at the Two Harbors SA station, home of the coldest men's room west of the Mississippi, where refrigerant must run through the urinals, and buy a pack of Marlboro Lights that we'll smoke three of and let the rest turn dry and dangerous on a windowsill at the cabin. And then, though it takes grit, you forge past that veritable wonderland of Carborundum, the 3M Sandpaper Museum, then past railroad cars and lighthouses that chug and shine as bed-and-breakfasts, through the 1,400 feet of the Silver Creek Tunnel, where you gotta beep, beeeep, beeeeeeep, and past Betty's Pies. Past Gooseberry Falls.

And you focus your eyes for deer in November, when the males are thinking more about romance than the prospect of bucking through your windshield at sixty-five miles per hour. Through towns almost dead, then resuscitated by hikers and snowmobilers, past Split Rock Lighthouse, the subject of more photos than Angelina Jolie, past the two 10-foot-tall Adirondack chairs in front of the Cove Point Resort, where seven out of ten tourists stop and sit to have their photo taken, and on along this road voted "one of the nation's premier byways," though anyone who's driven it doesn't need to see the trophy. Past the 320-foot cliffs of Palisade Head, where Macaulay Culkin in *The Good Son* dangled while his mom hemmed and hawed, and past Tettegouche State Park and the Jehovah's Witnesses Kingdom Hall, where, if the size of the parking lot is any indication of souls saved, they better wear out a little more shoe leather. Then 100 feet before the mile marker you begin craning your neck to glance downhill to see if any tragedy has befallen the cabin — a fire, a burglary, a slide into the lake — then scratch for the key under a flat rock, undo the padlock for the chain across the driveway and head down, staying hard left because a slide to the right means a 300-foot tumble down cliffs, not a good way to start a weekend, then leap from the truck, breathe deep, and smile.

IX

Buying
CABIN PARTS

*Keep an open mind —
you never know what might crawl in.*

ASK PEOPLE TO NAME THEIR FAVORITE childhood book, and many
will say *Charlotte's Web, The Little Engine That Could,* or *The Cat
in the Hat.* I remember not entire books but a single chapter from a
Pippi Longstocking book. In this chapter Pippi starts a "Thingfinders
Club." The only rule of membership is that when you find an item in
the street — a large bolt, an apron pocket, a bicycle reflector, a hub-
cap — you save it and turn it into something fun or fantastic. I'm still a
card-carrying member of the Thingfinders Club.

There are few things that hit my pleasure center more swiftly than
a unique, inexpensive, and (at least potentially) useful find, whether it's
in the street, online, or at an estate sale. I've had things tucked between
the studs and rafters of our garages for twenty years — an oak swinging
half-door from a men's room stall, ancient moldings, four stair spindles
hung over from a job completed years ago, boxes labeled MISC. NAILS,
old light fixtures. If you belong to the Thingfinders Club, I don't need to
extend the list — you know what's on it.

This is not a Johnny-come-lately compulsion. When I was in college,
walking from apartment to classroom, I rescued the round window
from the door of a junked Maytag dryer and kept it in my possession
for fifteen years, moving it twelve times. Not having land, financing, a
design, or even a burning urge to build a home, I knew I at least had a
cheap, interesting, and presumably heat-resistant window.

Part of this thriftiness is genetic. I've watched my mother, eighty years old, self-made, bad back, in Gucci heels, bend over to pick up a penny in our driveway, amazed that she can even straighten back up under the weight of her diamond tennis bracelet. Brought up poor, working to support her mother while in high school, when society was still trembling from the aftershock of the Great Depression, she knows the value of a penny.

My father's thriftiness was more time based. He didn't buy much, but when he did, he struck with cobralike quickness. When an encyclopedia salesman came to our door, before he got out the "Do you know that children in families with encyclopedias get higher grades than those that don't" speech, my father was writing the check. Didn't even know about the free atlas of the world. He did all his Christmas shopping on Christmas Eve. Though a lawyer and firmly ensconced in the upper middle class, he bought only one new car in his life, that in a special package deal that involved picking it up at the factory in Detroit.

And it's generational. My mother's mother, who lived with us, used to pilfer little plastic tubs of jelly from restaurants. I know this weighed heavily on her Catholic-value conscience but assume she found peace in rationalizing she was only delaying consumption. When we sorted through her room after she died, we found hundreds of jelly packets in the bottom of her underwear drawer, in shoeboxes, in the pockets of a housecoat — signs of a virtual jellyholic. When we helped my other grandmother move, we discovered a cache of over a hundred turkey wishbones. I come from thrifty stock.

The other half of my bargain-collecting impulses come from my addictive nature. I just love the flea-market rush.

So when it comes time to build, my "finding stuff" radar is fully activated. We have the time and flexibility, so we can build backward a little — find materials, then design the structure around those things. We not only save thousands but wind up with materials with character and history. Even some of the wood we use has stories to tell.

Wood you buy today at Home Depot or your local lumberyard is cut from thirty-year-old trees, planted and harvested like corn. It's the arboreal equivalent of steroid-pumped chicken; bland, predictable, but unarguably functional. But old wood that's been cut from virgin timber is rich, luxurious, experienced. The virgin white pine that once covered most of northern Minnesota grew for 100, 200, 300 years and big around as tollbooths. If you read the growth rings you discover stories of droughts, lightning strikes, and glory days. Old wood has had a chance to mellow like a fine whiskey, acquire a patina, and exude the rich aura of an old master's painting. So I keep dragging piles of old wood home.

We know we want large exposed beams to support the loft, so I keep my eyes open. I learn a salvage company is dismantling buildings at the Twin Cities Arsenal, a sprawling complex where bombs, bullets, torpedoes, and armaments had been manufactured from World War I to Vietnam. I carefully weigh the karma of the timbers. Do we want beams that have sheltered shrapnel, firebombs, and Bouncing Betties? I feel the beams are most heavily weighted on the side of righteousness and buy ten beams, 4 by 12 inches and 16 feet long, at forty dollars each; five for the floor beams, two for the stair jacks, and three for the exposed ceiling cross ties.

Some are painted, others are gray from old age; to the unimagined eye they're just plain ugly. Kat accepts these homely timbers with a leap of faith, trusting me when I tell her that beauty lies beneath the crud. I spend two to three hours on each beam, shaving away the outer skin with an electric hand planer. I love it in a way only a wood junkie can understand. Each swipe of the plane is like chopping open a geode; you don't know what's beyond the outer shell. I find impossible knots, gorgeous burls, grain figure that dances.

I come to a section on one beam signed, "Bud Wilhomen, The Guckenheimer Kid" in crayon and can't get myself to run the plane across it. Eighty years ago a carpenter signed this beam as an act of pride and immortality, and I'll be damned if I'm going to plane that away. Later on when we install this beam in the cabin, the Guckenheimer Kid's signature becomes a topic of hot contention. Kat doesn't love the idea of the Guckenheimer Kid's signature and surrounding patch of unplaned timber staring down into the kitchen. I do. It brings to a head one of our major differences: I love the quirky and the odd; Kat, the organized and predictable.

When Dick sees the Guckenheimer Kid's signature, he howls. He tells us Guckenheimer was a whiskey made long ago. Ha, here is even more history. It makes me want to leave the signature even more. The Guckenheimer signature stands unscathed and unplaned through most of the project. Then comes the moment of truth; Kat is sanding and applying polyurethane to the beams. Will we immortalize the crayoned name under three layers of clear finish — or sand it away? I realize I've made a strategic error in the placement of the beam. If I'd positioned it in a different part of the cabin I might have a stronger argument for preservation. But the Guckenheimer Kid is overlooking the kitchen — clearly Kat's domain. We both dig in our heels, but I can already tell Kat's got her spurs on. After living, loving, and arguing with someone for seven years, you know when you're going to lose an argument, even if you win the first round. The resistance is all window dressing, a mere marker for future negotiations. "Okay, I'll trade you one Guckenheimer Kid signature for one section of deck rail made from gnarly branches." Deal closed. We preserve the Guckenheimer Kid's memory with the digital camera and break out the belt sander.

There are places where you can buy reclaimed timber, cut to size, planed, and ready to go. But the cost is scandalous. Within the Duluth harbor sits the Duluth Timber Company; their motto is "Harvesting the Industrial Forest," and that's exactly what they do. They buy the salvage rights to old warehouses, wine vats, and water towers; dismantle them timber by timber; load them on barges; and ship them up through the Great Lakes to their mill. Driving in, you pass through a quarter mile of horizontal forest with a few deteriorating boats thrown in for good measure. Some timbers are 24 by 24 inches in girth and 30 feet long, cut from trees that might have taken a bullet in the Revolutionary War or witnessed Pilgrims landing. There are dismantled pickle barrels made from old-growth cypress, 5-foot-wide slabs of redwood cut from stumps found in California farm fields. They even have the bulk of the wood from the Twin Cities Arsenal where we bought the Guckenheimer Kid beams — but with a price tag of four times what we paid.

It would not be an unusual biography for the timbers stacked in the yard to have taken seed in Maine in the 1600s, been cut, then milled and transported to Boston in the 1800s, where they faithfully supported hundreds of tons of grain in a warehouse for ninety years, after which they were dismantled and shipped to Duluth, resawn and planed, then shipped to the West Coast to become cross ties in a million-dollar timber frame home overlooking Puget Sound. These timbers are part of history; you simply can't buy, find, or grow timbers of that stature any more. The stuff just doesn't grow on trees.

Trees can teach us something about ourselves. Different woods excel at different things, depending on their personalities. Windsor chair makers use a variety of woods: hickory for spindles because of its strength; ash for the hooped back because of its bendability; basswood for the contoured seat because of its availability in thick, wide planks; and maple for the legs because its fine grain is easy to work with on the lathe. You can flip-flop the roles of these woods, but a true craftsman understands the strengths and weaknesses of his woods and uses them wisely. He could try to force these woods to be something they're not, but why?

We can grab a lesson from that. We need to take time to find out what species we are; what our natural strengths and weaknesses are. Rather than going against the grain to be something we're not, maybe we should let ourselves grow in a more natural direction. We should be better craftsmen of our own lives.

———

A typical floor constructed with 2×10s spaced every 16 inches can be sheathed with ½- or ¾-inch plywood. It doesn't matter what this plywood looks like since it's concealed by carpeting above and drywall below. But with exposed beams, the boards that create the floor also create the ceiling for the rooms below. One man's ceiling is another man's floor. We need something that looks good and — since our beams are spaced every 3 feet — something substantial. I find what we're looking for in a field littered with 2×8 tongue-and-groove pine salvaged from the floor of an old brewery. It's been stored carelessly; for every good board I stack in the back of my truck I sort out ten rotting ones. I almost feel like I should apologize to the boards that don't make the cut; they're at the end of the trail.

At fifty cents a board foot, the pine is cheaper than plywood, but it's labor intensive to revive. I scan each board with a Radio Shack treasure hunting metal detector to find concealed nails. Removing the paint and grayness involves running each side of each board three or four times through my little portable planer. It's loud as hell, and I imagine myself sucking in lead paint particles as fast as my lungs and bloodstream can absorb them. I need to change planer blades every dozen boards or so, which essentially doubles the cost of the wood. Where a plywood floor would have gone down in an hour, this takes eight. But when we look up between the beams we find wood of stature and character to match the beams.

There are no local lumberyards, and those forty-five miles away in Grand Marais and Two Harbors are expensive and don't carry everything we need. We buy most of the lumber, plywood, shingles, fasteners, insulation, drywall, and siding materials from a home center in Duluth. Even with the eighty-five-dollar delivery charge, the prices are irresistibly lower. We buy the materials we need when they go on sale, then have them delivered when we need them. Two dollars off the price of a sheet of plywood is no big deal, but two dollars off each of eighty sheets is.

The truck driver is less than thrilled about backing down our driveway of death with a full load of lumber. On the first load he hollers down the driveway that he's gonna "dump it at the top." No way I'm reloading and lugging four tons of lumber down a 300-foot driveway. I flash him a twenty like a big shot to a maître d' in an overbooked restaurant. He creeps his way down. We repeat this bribe-and-drive ritual four times over the summer.

⊢————⊣

Just as eyes are the windows to the soul, windows add soul to a dwelling. They provide character and light — as well as a healthy dent in the checkbook. We know we want lots of light. We know we want big doors overlooking the lake. We know we want arched or circular windows to add to the cottage look. So we know we have to scrounge.

The first find — a 9-foot-wide patio door — comes via the good old-fashioned classifieds. The asking price is $400, about one-sixth of the cost of a new door. Here I come. The gleaming white door has a history. It's been cratered in a hailstorm. The guy selling it is the contractor who'd replaced it. He's also an auto-body repairman, and he's put those skills to work on the door. He's sanded it down, filled the dents with Bondo, sanded the surface, applied primer, then sprayed the door with auto-body enamel. I can tell from the restored Willys Jeep the door is leaning against that the guy is a perfectionist. I buy it and tuck $2,000 into a mythical savings account.

The large round-top window in the bedroom loft comes from a window display closeout sale at a home center. The $1,200 window has been marked down to $300. We negotiate that down to $150, then take another ten percent off by opening a charge account. The mythical savings account grows.

I purchase a stained-glass window with a parrot (toucan, if you're feeling tropical) on it that had once graced a local bar. At sixty bucks it's irresistible. Building the frame and trim for it consumes a weekend and ten jigsaw blades, but it greets us every time we climb the stairs.

When Home Depot runs a promotion offering "10% off the price of any purchase over $1,000 when you open a charge account" — another charge account — we do just that, then buy the rest of the windows. We decide to splurge on two Gothic arch windows, one nestled into the gable end overlooking the lake, the other nestled into the peak opposite that. Anything not square in the window world is subject to highway robbery. But there's no other way. The fancy-pants grills that divide the windows into smaller arched panes cost more than my first car.

———————

We even import some materials. While vacationing in Maui, we fall in love with a porcelain bathroom sink, decorated with frolicking fish and dolphins in primary colors. We buy a hammered metal mermaid with copper-wire hair and two fish with Marilyn Monroe lips at the same time. The fish and mermaid we ship, but since we haven't reached our luggage quota for the return trip home, we decide to save the hundred-dollar shipping charge and check the seventy-pound sink like normal baggage. Along with a case of pineapple.

Depending on the story you choose to believe, an hour over the Pacific the left engine of our plane is either (a) hit by lightning or (b) receives a jolt of static electricity that had built up around the nose of the plane. Either way, the engine fries. With a third of our horsepower in cardiac arrest, the pilot turns back for Honolulu. The worst part isn't dumping thousands of gallons of jet fuel into the Pacific to lighten the plane for landing. It isn't the roller-coaster ride back. It isn't landing on a runway lined with fire trucks and ambulances. It isn't even the claw marks Kat leaves on my thigh. The worst part is lugging the damn seventy-pound sink, the case of pineapple, and our luggage around for the next thirty-six hours.

We haul the sink from the luggage conveyer belt to the bus that drives us to the hotel where the airline puts us up for the night. We haul it up the thirty concrete stairs to the hotel entrance, into our room, back down the stairs a few hours later to the taxi that takes us to the airport, back to the luggage check-in. That airplane is three hours late in taking off, and when a passenger who'd been on the aborted flight the night before goes into hysterics over the probability of another mishap, there's another delay while the plane taxies back to the terminal to deposit her. We miss our connecting flight in LA, so we lug seventy pounds' worth of sink along with our luggage and case of pineapple around for another night of cab rides, hotels, and check-ins.

The irony is the artist who made the sink had painted it in Oregon and shipped it to Hawaii. It's the best damn traveled bathroom sink in the annals of aviation or building history. But it's ensconced in the bathroom at Oma Tupa, Oma Lupa, unbroken and rich in history. The pineapple didn't fare as well.

And so it goes. The cabinet for the bathroom sink is a revamped 1950s dining room serving table. The kitchen cabinets are from bleacher seats salvaged from a local high school. (If you ever need to know how to get bubble gum off planer blades, I'm the one to ask.) The wood for the deck is 200-year-old clear redwood salvaged from a house I remodeled 12 years ago. In a land where over a quarter of the space in landfills is occupied by construction scraps and demolished buildings, recycling building parts is a good thing. Oma Tupa has done her part.

X

Skin
OF THE CABIN
&
MIDDLE-AGE BLAHS

Beauty is only plywood deep.

I F DESIGNING A CABIN IS AKIN to conception and driving the last nail is tantamount to retiring, then somewhere in between comes middle age. It's that stage where the excitement of planning has passed, the direction has been established, yet the finish is a long way off. It is yeoman service: hard, straightforward, monotonous work. It's staining and putting up siding, installing shingles, finishing the little details that were so easy to put off earlier. There's no Viagra made for these tasks. One day looks an awful lot like the next. There are regrets and things you'd change, but at this point, for the most part, the course is set. It's nose to the grindstone.

Getting the windows and doors installed will give the cabin — and us — a sense of shelter and stability. Being closed in will mean we're safe from rain, sleet, and snow. Also from, strange as it sounds, building material bandits. Windows and doors on a "per square inch" basis are among the most expensive materials in a cabin. Many are the tales of windows being delivered, stacked in the garage, only to disappear that night. My insurance agent told me about one contractor who installed a pair of expensive arched-top windows the day they were delivered so *that* wouldn't happen; pry bar–wielding construction pirates removed them and hauled them away that night. If you think standing guard will solve the problem, you're wrong. One homeowner pitched a tent on the job site to prevent theft. He ran to the store one afternoon and returned to find . . . drum roll here . . . his tent and Coleman stove missing.

But if your windows and doors don't walk, if you've framed the rough openings so they're square and the right size, the windows and doors go in bam, bam, bam. We muster the troops: the full contingent of kids and a miscellaneous boyfriend. Maggie and Sarah staple Tyvek — a special paper that's equivalent to a house windbreaker — around the window openings. Everyone else starts hauling windows and setting ladders. The small windows go in easily. One person hoists them into place from the outside. Another on the inside, with a level and wood shims, squares and centers the window in the opening. A nod of the head signals the okay to nail the window in place through the exterior fins. It's hoist, adjust, nod, and bang. The large bank of three windows above the patio door falls into the same installation rhythm but requires three extension ladders, three grunting bodies and a one-two-three coordinated effort to lift it in place. The windows enhance the look of the cabin, yet diminish the size of the openings to which we've become accustomed. A 20-by-30-inch "air window" is reduced to a 15-by-25-inch glass window because of the frame and sash. Plus suddenly, nature becomes "out there"; there's a barrier. Prior to installing windows you're working outside, even if you're working inside.

Amid all the window activity, the shingles and tar paper are delivered. Again I have to lure the truck driver down the driveway of death with a twenty-dollar gratuity. We unload the three tons of shingles by hand and stack them on the ground.

Minutes after the truck leaves, John, who I've known since junior high, pops in while his wife is at a seminar in Ely. Somewhere in his haste to turn his Jeep around, he misjudges his whereabouts. Two right wheels go over the steep embankment; the Jeep readies itself for the

200-foot cartwheel into the lake. The scenario has catastrophe written all over it. John puts in a gold medal performance in the "grab the dog and catapult out the passenger side door" competition. He dusts himself off, then looks around in hopes no one has seen this ham-fisted move. No such luck. The Jeep lists so far downhill that it defies physics. It would be bad feng shui — a very bad example of the "art of placement" — to have a Jeep parked in the lake. But some greater power — God or gravity — keeps a finger against the side of the Jeep, and the embankment holds.

By sheer providence I'm driving a truck of titanic proportions with a winch on the front that Ford has loaned to the editors of the magazine to use for a promotional stint. But before we can extract the Jeep from death's teeter-totter, we gotta move the shingles that are in the way. Guys being guys, it's, "Well, if you can fling an eighty-pound bundle of shingles over your shoulder, so can I."

"Oh, you carried two at once? Screw this hernia and bad back; watch this!" When we're done, we all slowly drift in different directions so the others can't see how hard we're panting and trying to catch our breath.

We connect the winch to the Jeep and start winding. I imagine the Jeep sliding out of control, pulling the truck along with it down and over the embankment; two climbers connected by a safety rope which, rather than saving both, pulls both to their deaths. After a few twitchy moments the Jeep is on solid ground.

We decide to stain the siding before it goes up. Rolling stain onto sheets of siding lying horizontally on sawhorses is *way* easier than rolling it on vertically while you're perched 16 feet in the air on an extension ladder. We decide to do it right, which means priming both sides, then applying two coats of stain to the front. By priming both sides, then standing the 4-by-8-foot sheets of siding against trees, we can work without having to wait for one side to dry. We've tinted the primer blue so the topcoats of stain don't have to cover bright white. At the end of the day forty sheets of blue plywood siding dot the woods. The landscape looks like a Christo sculpture on acid.

Kat oversees quality control of our domestic workforce, while I get other things ready. I may be lifting more, but her job clearly requires more management skills. The kids get the notion that this is their cabin, too; that hard work will not only push the project along faster but also secure cabin usage rights in the future. At first, our neatest daughters try to keep their clothes paint free — they have to look cool, even when painting in the wilderness. But after the first few splatters, it becomes clear their clothes are beyond recovery. Pretty soon they're having roller fights; warring with oil-based stain and primer. Everyone has streaked blue punk rock hair, a sort of northwoods Blue Man Group. We go through two gallons of mineral spirits cleaning bodies and brushes.

Katie — Kat's Pekingese that came with the marriage — hangs in there through it all. The breed originated in China, where they served as companions and protectors for the imperial court. They were treated as royalty; commoners had to bow to them. Katie knows all this. To show her fierce protective side she darts off the deck to chase an occasional chipmunk. Having performed her duties, she returns and waits for us to lift her back onto the deck. She gives that little head tilt. "Excuse me, I've already been waiting seven whole seconds here." It's all in a day.

———

Bruce, the woodworker who'd helped us get the rafters in place, comes up the next weekend. From the furniture he creates you can tell he's a ten on the perfectionist scale. You need X-rays to find the fasteners in his work — if he uses them at all. Bruce's cedar strip canoe looks nicer than most dining room tables. When he fillets a walleye he's landed from it, it's like he's transplanting a cornea.

So I know his work will be five star. He cuts loose on making the trim for the exterior of the windows. The top pieces have a slight arch.

The week before, when I created the trim above the entry door, I took a thin scrap of wood, bent it in a rough arc, traced the outline onto the cedar board, traced around a pint paint can to establish the round ends, and cut the thing out with a jigsaw. I rounded the edges with a router and in twenty minutes, *bam*, I'm done.

Bruce does not operate in this seat-of-the-pants world. He asks me where my band saw is (don't have one), where my planer is (see that rusted thing under the sawhorses?), where my miter box is (at home in the garage). He half-jokingly, half-seriously asks me how he can create trim without these essentials. He is a woodworker; I'm a carpenter. We both work wood, but the way we approach it, and the tools we use, differ greatly.

So he creates his own miniworkshop from the crude tools at hand. He creates a workbench from two sawhorses and concocts a vice from a couple of Quik-Grip clamps. He traces, cuts, planes, sands, routs, test fits, fine tunes, sands a little more, then predrills holes, and tacks the trim in place using finish nails. He stands back, takes 'em down, and shapes them a hair differently. Each piece is perfect. In the end, few will notice the difference between my seat-of-the-pants arches and Bruce's picture-perfect ones, but that's simply the way we work.

Laying shingles is like laying sod; the materials are heavy, the actions are mechanical, the payoff is rapid. You see progress by the minute. However, unlike laying sod — where the biggest mistake you can make is green side down — a mistake shingling can land you a quadriplegic, even a dead quadriplegic. Shingling involves high-altitude tasks, heavy materials, and tall ladders; not a great combination. Ladders falling over, kicking out, hitting a power line, or falling on you will injure you quicker than any other building task. Statistically, the chances of ladder injuries are greatest if you're (1) male (can't help that much), (2) between the ages of fifteen and sixty-four (can't help that much), (3) on a ladder set at the wrong angle so the bottom can kick out (that I can help).

There aren't that many true ladder accidents. There are hurry-dents, there are stupi-dents, there are reaching-too-far-past-the-side-rail-dents. But most accidents don't have to happen. One second can change your life when you're on a ladder — and that change is rarely for the good. A friend of mine who'd painted house interiors for twenty years reached a little too far to dab a spot he'd missed near the ceiling and is now in a wheelchair for the rest of his life.

So I'm near-paranoid when it comes to ladder safety. When working from the deck, I screw a big cleat to the deck to keep the legs from kicking out. When I'm working from earth, I make sure the spurs on the bottom of the ladder are pointing down and digging in firmly. I make sure there's nothing mooshy under foot. When I get to the top, I spend a minute securing the top of the ladder to the eaves with a chunk of rope.

Roof pitches are measured in terms of $x/12$ pitches. A 4/12 pitch is a roof that rises 4 inches vertically for every 12 inches it runs horizontally. This is an 18-degree angle, the angle of many ramblers and ranch homes. A 12/12 pitch is a 45-degree slant. That's what Oma Tupa has. It's formidable.

Shingling a single-story home with a 4/12 pitch is a walk in the park, albeit a hilly one. The nine steps up the ladder, even with an eighty-pound bundle of shingles draped over your shoulder, is short and sweet. You can plop shingles, rolls of tar paper, nails, and your chalk box on the roof, and they stay put. By twisting your ankles you can walk up, down, and across the roof without much fear of sliding. A world-class roofer, with air equipment, good knees, and someone feeding him shingles from above can install three or four squares of shingles (a square being 100 square feet of shingles) an hour, all day long.

As the roof pitch and wall height increase, so does the level of shingling difficulty. It requires more shingles, more tar paper, more nails, more time, more cohones, more roof brackets, and taller ladders to get you where you need to go and stay there.

I go at it. While shingling I also install the barge rafters that support the eaves — putzy work. And the siding for the dormers. Putzy work. As long as I have roof brackets set, I use my little electric paint sprayer to paint the underside of the roof plywood on the eaves. More putzy work. There's flashing to install, a couple of skylights to put in, a chimney to erect for the woodstove. Putzy, putzy. There's a ridge vent to install for venting the roof. When I'm working on the downhill side of the cabin

Installing the chimney, skylight, shingles, and dormers involved lots of high-altitude work and sore muscles.

I'm 25 feet above the ground, which is pushing the limits of my comfort level. Each trip up the ladder takes its toll on my knees and nerves. My progress is glacial.

For high-altitude work you need redundancy for safety; if your main means of support breaks, tilts, or cuts loose, you need a secondary way of preventing yourself from plummeting. If one leg of your ladder suddenly sinks into a soft spot, the rope you've used to secure the top to the rafters buys you a little thinking time. If an upper roof bracket gives way, the set of brackets below will catch you. The ultimate in safety is a harness system similar to what mountain climbers wear. Harnesses can be lifesaving, but they're a hassle to use; the rope gets in the way, they're ball pinchers, you need to unclick yourself each time you go down the ladder. I borrow one from work, never wear the actual harness, but secure the safety rope at the peak so I have something right in front of me to grab in case something busts loose. Plus I keep my cell phone on my hip. When Kat asks, "Are you being careful?" I respond, "Careful? My safety harness is right here."

A typical fifteen minutes goes like this: break open a bundle of shingles, grab 1-2-3-4-5-6-7-8-9-10 shingles, climb the extension ladder (chib, chib, chib, chib, chib, chib, chib, chib, chib, chib, chib, chib), crawl onto the roof brackets, connect the gun to the hose (phhhhip), position a shingle and nail it in place (pht, pht, pht, pht), grab and nail another shingle (pht, pht, pht, pht), grab and nail another shingle (pht, pht, pht, ph—), oops — outa nails, climb down the ladder (chib, chib, chib, chib, chib, chib, chib, chib, chib, chib, chib, chib), stick 1-2-3 coils of nails in my pouch, grab 1-2-3-4-5-6 more shingles while I'm at it, then back up the ladder (chib, chib, chib, chib, chib, chib, chib, chib, chib, chib, chib, chib), shimmy back onto the roof jacks, cut a shingle to fit (shhhhhwip), then pht, pht, pht, pht; damn, those didn't sink all the way, take out the hammer and whap, whap, whap, whap, and pht, pht, pht, pht, oops — outa shingle tin flashing (chib, chib, chib, chib, chib, chib, chib, chib, chib, chib, chib, chib) — and if you think it's boring and tedious reading this, try doing it.

After a solid week of fifty-trips-up-and-down-the-ladder-per-day, I've had it. I've got all the weird stuff done, skylights in, flashing installed. My knees are shot, the fingers that aren't calloused are blistered. I feel mule kicked. My knees are considering going on strike. I pull out a scrap of paper my friend John has given me with the name of a shingler who lives up the road. I pick up the phone (dit, dit, dit, dit, dit, dit, dit). Yah, he can finish the job this Saturday (aaaaaaaaah). When he's done I write a check (scrib, scrib, scribble). Then the sounds of silence.

Installing the siding takes just as long hourwise as shingling, but since the cabin is weathertight with or without it, there's less urgency. We're going for the quaint seaside board-and-batten look. It involves installing 4-by-8-foot sheets of rough-sawn plywood, then nailing vertical 1-by-2-inch cedar battens every 12 inches on top. Because the cabin is small, with lots of windows, doors, and dormers, every piece involves measuring, cutting, fitting, recutting, then re-recutting. A few pieces are squarish, shaped like Wyoming, but most are shaped like Nevada doing a headstand. Or Georgia. Some pieces have an angled cut on top to accommodate the roof pitch, a notch on the side to accommodate a window, and a cutout near the bottom to accommodate an electrical box. For these I measure and sketch little pictures on scraps of wood or on masking tape I keep stuck to the side of my tape measure, then plot out the geometric puzzle, cut, and pray.

We get the plywood siding installed, then, starting on the back of the cabin, install the battens at 12-inch intervals; at least from the driveway it looks done. Some friends come up the following spring to help finish the siding. It's been so long since I installed the first batch of battens that I forget the 12-inch spacing, and we install the remainder at 16-inch intervals. If I were a contractor building this for a customer, I'd have to fix it. But I don't think these customers will mind.

XI

A
Superior Lake

(SOME SUPERIOR
TOWNS)

When you get caught with your pants down,
run like hell.

I F YOU WERE TO STICK THE POINT of a compass in the middle of Oma
Tupa and swing a two-mile radius, you wouldn't find much in the
way of retail or entertainment. You'd encircle a small store where AAA
batteries and mosquito spray, two essentials for northern Minnesota
survival, cost the same as a good bottle of wine. There's a small resort
with a building converted into the Illgen Jail, complete with stuffed
cloth prisoners poking their heads through the bars. There's the
Fish Out of Water (because that's how the big city owners felt before
opening it) Gift Shop. You'd find a road that leads you to the 200-mile
Superior Hiking Trail. And of course, you'd find a lot of lake.

East and West Coasters may snicker, but we Midwesterners lay claim to
Lake Superior as our ocean. It is oceanlike in its immensity, in its dan-
gerousness, in its variety, and in its ability to inspire. It lacks only the
saltiness and cruise ship debris.

The fact is, 1.1 billion years ago, Lake Superior was a single gigan-
tic-shift-in-the-tectonic-plates away from becoming a saltwater ocean.
The entire northern portion of what is now the United States began
parting ways with the rest of the country. The land separated as if
a gigantic zipper — with the pull starting at the tip of Superior and
the teeth extending along what is now the course of the Mississippi

River — began unzipping. It was on its way to dividing the USA into two continents, with ocean in between, when the zipper snagged somewhere around Nebraska, and Mother Nature pulled her zipper back up over the next few million years in an act of geologic modesty.

During this time Mother Nature tossed and turned. Lava oozed. Minerals crystallized into gemstones such as amethyst and greenstone. Agates, Mother Nature's surprise in the Cracker Jack box, were created. Basalt amassed in such quantities that its iron content can swing a compass 50 degrees off course and its density can increase the pull of gravity to the point where it can affect one's energy level during a long hike in some areas. Volcanic activity, sedimentation, upheaval, glaciers, and erosion kept stirring the pot.

About 10,000 years ago, a blink of an eye in earth science measures, the last ice age went into recession. Vast amounts of water were trapped in the deep indentations left behind. Five massive lakes — great lakes to be exact — each resembling a gourd left in the backseat of a car on a sweltering day, were created. These squiggly lakes, a cartographer's nightmare, eventually created much of the border between what is now the United States and Canada — and the shoreline upon which Oma Tupa sits.

Lake Superior holds ten percent of the world's available fresh water: over three quadrillion gallons. If you throw in the other four Great Lakes, this freshwater monopoly increases to twenty percent. When mathematicians try to put Superior's vastness into concrete terms, they come up with images such as these:

- It contains enough water to flood all of North and South America beneath 12 inches of water.
- You'd need to mix 6.4 quadrillion cups of Tang into Lake Superior to give it the proper flavor.

- If you let the water drain through its natural outlets, it would take 191 years to empty.

Superior is 383 miles long and 160 miles across at its widest point. Its 32,000-square-mile surface area is equal to that of Maine. If you traversed all the coves and points that compose the shoreline, your pedometer would read 2,980 miles. If you lowered the Freedom Tower into the deepest part of Superior, only the top four floors, plus the satellite needle, would be visible.

By surface area it's the world's largest lake. By volume only Lake Tanganyika in Africa and Lake Baikal in Russia contain more water. Superior is so vast that — like the oceans — it doesn't merely affect the weather, it creates it. The average winter temperature of the water is 40 degrees; in summer it warms up 1 or 2 balmy degrees. The notion that Superior "never gives up her dead" is based in fact; the microorganisms that cause bodies to bloat and float can't survive the frigid waters.

Lake-effect snows can dump 22 inches on the shore and none a mile inland. On an average of once every twenty years the lake freezes over, though "freezing over" is a misnomer. It merely becomes logjammed with a mass of ever-shifting ice floes. Residents of Madeline Island can drive the two miles across the ice to Bayfield, Wisconsin, on a Monday, only to discover stretches of open water blocking their return on Wednesday. An acquaintance who winters on the island keeps two railroad spikes ganged together with rope on his dashboard, so if he breaks through, he at least has a prayer of grabbing them, busting out a window and clawing himself back onto the ice. A two-story home sits on the bottom of Superior between Madeline Island and Bayfield, the victim of an overconfident house mover and an underconfident ice pack.

Four million tourists visit Superior annually, but the lake has a much larger working side. It's been used for transportation, shipping, and commercial fishing for hundreds of years. Massive ships — the largest measuring 1,013 feet in length and 100 feet in width — help provide scale. The *Titanic*, by comparison, was 882 feet long. Many ships are driven at the breakneck speed of 16 to 20 miles per hour by pairs of gigantic diesel engines sporting twenty cylinders and 20,000 horsepower.

You can halfway guess where people hail from by what they call these monsters. If they call them "boats" — which is something that can be taken out of the water — they're most likely inlanders. If they call them "ships," there's a pretty good chance they're from a coastal state. If the word "freighters" rolls off their tongue, there's a pretty good shot they've spent some time in a port town somewhere. But if they say, "Look at that laker!" you're listening to someone who lives within spitting distance of a Great Lakes port.

Regardless of what you call them — ships, freighters, lakers — nothing that floats is a match for the Great Lakes when they're in a bad mood. Fall puts the lakes in their foulest temperament. As with hurricanes the largest storms are given names, and some are legendary.

In November of 1913 the weeklong "Great Storm" on Lake Huron sank ten vessels, ran twenty more ashore, and claimed two hundred and thirty-five lives. In terms of lives lost and intensity, most people mark it as the worst storm to ever strike the Great Lakes. It was reported that 60-mile-per-hour winds blew for 16 hours straight, creating waves 35 feet high.

The 1905 "Blow" on Superior took out thirty ships, including the *William Edenborn*, which was smashed ashore at Split Rock twenty miles south of Oma Tupa. In another horrific episode during the same storm, 40,000 citizens of Duluth watched helplessly from shore in the 13-degrees-below-zero cold as the 430-foot *Mataafa* was smashed in two against the rocks. The lake too rough and the distance too far to attempt a rescue, people manned their bonfires along the shore that night, then chopped nine dead from the icy grasp of Superior the next morning.

The storm that took down the fabled *Edmund Fitzgerald* on November 10, 1975, was no sissy. When the "Fitz" was launched in 1958 it was the biggest object ever dropped into fresh water. It took waves of over 30 feet to destroy the 730-foot-long freighter. With no survivors the exact story behind her sinking will never be known. One thing is for certain — the boat went down fast, probably in less time than it took Gordon Lightfoot to run through his fourteen-verse song commemorating the tragedy.

None of these storms or tragedies are record holders in terms of sheer number of lives lost. That dubious distinction goes to the passenger liner *Eastland*, which capsized in the Chicago River within a stone's throw of shore on a calm, sunny Saturday morning in 1915. Eight hundred thirty-five people heading out for a pleasant excursion drowned when the boat rolled over in the harbor. Water ballast tanks that hadn't been filled made the boat unsteady to begin with. But, it's hypothesized that 2,500 passengers all shifting to the port side for some unclear reason may have made her barrel roll.

Many are the tales of small-scale fishermen doing hand-to-hand combat with Superior with predictably mixed results. On a miserable November day in 1958 — a day so wretched most people wouldn't even stand on the shoreline — Helmer Aakvik launched his small wooden skiff to go in search of Carl Hammer, his twenty-six-year-old neighbor and the man with whom he shared a boathouse, who'd gone missing. Aakvik, figuring Hammer's boat had developed mechanical problems, loaded an extra motor, gas, and an ax in his own boat and headed out to where Hammer usually set his nets, hoping the young man had tied off to one of the net buoys to await rescue. Hammer was nowhere to be found, so Aakvik cut his engine and let his own boat drift, hoping he would travel in the same direction as Hammer. The gale kept getting angrier and angrier. Aakvik's boat kept taking on water and ice. He threw the extra motor and gas overboard to lighten the load. When he kept sinking, he threw his own motor, gas, and everything else overboard. His hands were so cold he could no longer grip the oars, so he let his hands freeze to the handles so he could row. With no hands to chop ice, his feet froze to the bottom of the boat. He'd been out twenty-four hours when the Coast Guard found him — alive — and pried him out of his boat. Hammer was never found. When I overhear someone at the gym telling his buddy to "man up" by putting an extra ten pounds on the Cybex machine, I think of Helmer.

Lake Superior is a 32,000-square-mile Rorschach inkblot test, a singular thing that everyone perceives a little differently. Some people see it as a thing of action — they sail across it, wade into it, skip stones along it, pull fish out of it, scuba dive through it, surf over it. Others see it as a contemplative thing — they stare at it, write about it, sketch it, photograph it, nap next to it.

One stormy afternoon we head down to our beach with friends Tom and Nan. The northeast wind is driving the waves dead ahead into the thumper hole, creating plumes that crash 60 feet into the air. We all see different inkblots. Tom sees a science experiment and throws chunks of wood into the surf to see how they travel. Nan sees a chance to get her adrenaline going and creeps perilously close to the edge to watch the pounding. I see a percussion instrument and count waves to find what time it's beating to. Kat sees a photo op and clicks off pictures of the crashing and bashing. It's one lake, but we all see different things.

Not long ago someone looked over toward the thumper hole and saw something different yet — two moons rising over Superior. Kat and I had been installing siding on one of those days where the air was thick as a sauna. We needed refreshment, and Superior's 3 quadrillion gallons were calling. We scouted the beach from above to check for passing boaters or agate pickers. None. We clawed our way down the embankment and checked once again for humanity. None. We set up the towels and Dr. Bronner's "all-in-one-Jaweh" peppermint soap. Among a cluster of boulders we stripped and scrubbed. I only had on my flip-flops and Kat was two articles short of that.

Kat and I subscribe to differing schools of lake bathing. I am of the "lather and plunge" persuasion. Once you're soaped up head to toe, there's no turning back. You plunge. Kat uses the bed-bath technique; a little soap and water on the washrag, scrub a square foot of skin, rinse and repeat. In frigid Superior my approach is death by firing squad; Kat's approach, slower, like being drawn and quartered.

Kat, without glasses but radar fully extended, detected humanity on the beach. Since the beach is accessible only by water or one of the properties flanking it, we figured these were neighbors, one of whom, according to Dick, was a Methodist minister. This was not how we'd envisioned meeting the neighbors; we were thinking clothed would be more appropriate. Swimming out into the lake spelled sure hypothermia. We managed to get on skivvies, but that was it. We made a run for the border, scrambling up the hill, never looking back for fear of making eye contact. We've yet to meet the neighbors.

Scribe a larger circle around Oma Tupa, and you'll find three unique towns — Duluth, Grand Marais, and Ely — each robust in its own right.

Duluth at first glance looks like a dirt-under-the-fingernails industrial town — and while there's dirt under some of the nails, it's not under all. The city of a hundred thousand wraps its twelve-mile-long arms around the western tip of Superior. It's the eleventh busiest port in the United States, quite a claim for a town 2,300 miles from the Atlantic Ocean. Mile-long trains hauling taconite from the Iron Range, grain from North Dakota, and coal from Montana pass over 35W delivering their booty to the loading docks.

Beyond its hardcore infrastructure lies a town of surprising grace. It supports a symphony orchestra, a ballet troupe, three colleges, a minor league baseball team, the Bayport Blues Festival, Grandma's Marathon, and the world's largest freshwater aquarium.

Canal Park along the lake is now the epicenter of the artsy-touristy-gotta-see part of the city. Six-foot metal sturgeon spout water arcs across sidewalks, and horse-drawn carriages plod up and down the street. Lakewalk, a boardwalk made from teak, hugs the lake, then runs another 3 miles along the shore, passing sculptures, parks, and a Vietnam memorial that looks like a football helmet.

The aerial lift bridge in the harbor is the Eiffel Tower of the North — metallic, massive, awe-inspiring. A series of blasts and bells signals its intent to raise itself to all or part of its 120-foot height so a barge, ship, or catamaran mast can pass below. The maritime museum in its shadow is a wonderland for little kids and little kids at heart. It sports 12-foot-tall pistons from old freighters and an 11-ton, trampoline-size bronze propeller.

Grand Marais, fifty miles north of our cabin, is a small town packed with big diversity. SPAM-filled canoeists and vodka-filled yachtsmen rub elbows at the Angry Trout restaurant. There's a vibrant theater, music, and arts scene. The variety of courses offered through North House Folk School — northern bog ecology, Swedish Potato Sausage making, casket building — attests to the wide range of citizenry that call Grand Marais home. Over the course of the summer you can attend the Shakespeare, Scandinavian Music, Boreal Birding, and Summer Solstice Festivals. Citizens and tourists have banded together to keep the Burger Kings and Walmarts at bay, though a Subway was able to latch onto the outer fringes.

Nowhere else but on the Grand Marais public radio station can you get a play-by-play broadcast — complete with color commentary — of a dogsled race. The station has some of the best music programming on the planet — at least if you're a boomer: there are four straight hours of blues, a jazz hour, a Grateful Dead hour, and a program of contemporary bluegrass. The station is like the town — diverse, fun, a little odd.

Ely completes the triangle that surrounds our cabin. It's home to the International Wolf Center and gateway to the one-million-acre Boundary Waters Canoe Area Wilderness. It is aptly nicknamed "City Where the Wilderness Begins."

You can visit the Dorothy Molter Museum, the place that honors "The Root Beer Lady," who lived a solitary life in the BWCAW for fifty-six years; solitary, unless you count the 7,000 canoeists and campers that visited her a year. She brewed a wicked root beer using eight-gallon crocks, and cooled it right through August using ice she'd hand cut from the lake. Charles Kuralt visited her, *National Geographic* documented her, and two people wrote biographies of her. When the government banned private residences in the BWCAW in the 1970s, enough root beer lovers raised a stink so they let Dorothy stay. When they banned retail sales in the BWCAW, she gave her root beer away and people gave her "donations." Dorothy was a woman with some steel wool in her britches. After she died, volunteers disassembled her cabin log-by-log, hauled it to Ely via snowmobile and dogsled, then put it back together again. You can still guzzle one of her Isle of Pines root beers while sitting on a picnic table outside her relocated cabin.

Kat and I have watched eagles, wild turkey, fox, deer, raccoon, squirrels, and a dozen different types of birds cavort outside our living room window — in Stillwater, a stone's throw from the Twin Cities. There's not nearly as much diversity around Oma Tupa. There are deer aplenty — they sleep in the woods behind the cabin in the summer and bed down on the warmth of the septic tank come winter. Dick talks about having shot a troublemaking black bear out of a tree at the campground one night, quickly dispelling the notion in young campers' minds that bears are cute, wear neckties, and are mostly concerned about forest fires. Occasionally a moose with a lousy sense of direction will drift through the area. But most inhabitants have fins or feathers, with the feathered providing the most visible entertainment.

A pair of loons — their moniker derived from their loony stride — reside in the bay outside our door. Every spring we see the two, cruising around the bay with two or three rubber-ducky-size offspring, home schooling them in the ways of eating, diving, and being loony. The same backset legs that make them awkward on land make them torpedoes in the water, allowing them to dive 200 feet while holding their breath for up to five minutes. They're one of the few birds with solid bones, which aid their underwater velocity. Loons may also be loony because of their vulnerability to attack by land (raccoons and weasels), air (crows and eagles), and sea (muskies and pike). Though baby loons are precocial — able to swim and dive at birth — they often ride on a parent's back for protection. Minnesotans are so fond of them they've been designated the state bird. They have a number of distinct calls, one of which is often described as one of "maniacal laughter." Like all good Minnesotans, loons mate for life.

Seagulls also abound and are so numerous we've nicknamed the bus-size rock 50 feet offshore where they congregate "Seagull Rock." They're quirky things. If they could talk they'd sound like Gilbert Gottfried. As a group they've been known to stomp their feet in unison to simulate rain, thus tricking earthworms — one of their favorite snacks — to come to the surface. They're adaptable critters, too; a special gland above their eyes acts as a filter, allowing them to drink either fresh water or salt water. Just as pigeons have been branded "rats with wings," seagulls have been marked as "garbagemen with wings." The nickname comes from their propensity to eat anything and everything;

a plus, since they keep picnic areas, boat launches, and carcass-strewn beaches tidy.

A pair of bald eagles maintained a massive nest in the upper reaches of a nearby spruce until high winds took off the top of the tree. Their abode was not as impressive as some — they've found eagle nests 9 feet in diameter, 16 feet in height, weighing over 2 tons — but it had an undeniably commanding view. They still use the tree as their hunting shack; from it, the occupants — with eyesight four times keener than ours — can spot a fish a mile away, then, using their 7-foot wingspan, hit speeds of 100 miles per hour, to nab dinner with talons ten times stronger than the grip of a human. With their hooked beaks, paring knife–size talons, and perpetually pissed-off look, they create a foreboding presence. Nonetheless I've seen birds one-eighth their size engage this National Emblem in a dispute over culinary rights and win. They've been known to snatch already-caught food from osprey, otters, and, on occasion, unsuspecting fishermen. If you're an optimist you call this behavior "opportunistic." If you're Ben Franklin — no fan of old baldy — you call him a bird of "bad moral Character," that "does not get his Living honestly."

But whenever Kat and I see an eagle soar overhead we're certain it's a good omen — a manuscript will be accepted, good fortune will befall one of our kids . . . maybe the plumber will actually show up.

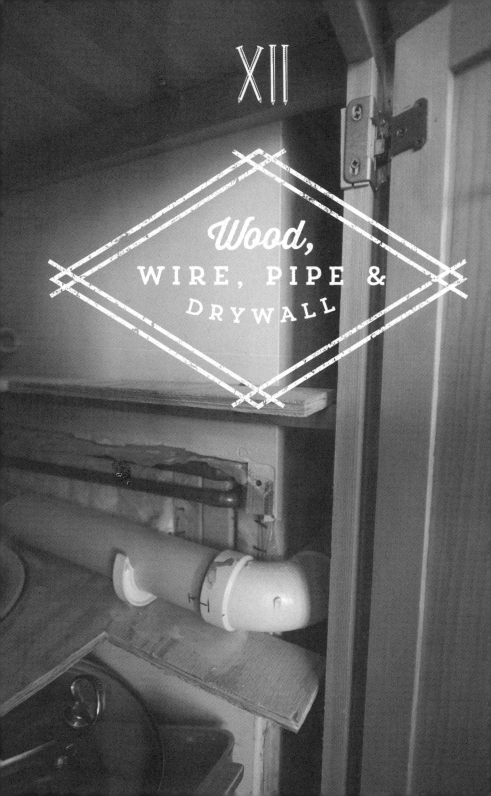

XII

Wood,
WIRE, PIPE &
DRYWALL

The quandary with life is you're halfway through before you realize it's a do-it-yourself project.

F OR FIFTEEN YEARS I DWELLED IN THE WORLD of carpentry, building, and remodeling. It's a melting pot of third-generation craftsmen, first-generation misfits, and everything in between. You find high school dropouts working alongside law-school graduates. There are those who grew up knowing they wanted to work in the trades and those, like me, who grabbed a summer job, then woke up ten years later, hammer still in hand.

Everyone has his or her own story. I once worked on a crew where four of the five of us had teaching degrees. One electrician I worked with had a degree in electrical engineering but opted for pulling wire versus pulling his hair out in an office. I built geodesic domes alongside the fellow who wound up teaching my daughter's high school concert choir. On any given job site you might find a nineteen-year-old laborer listening to hip-hop and a sixty-four-year-old journeyman tuned in to Rush Limbaugh. And it is this quilt of personalities that makes the construction site such an interesting place to dwell.

The saying goes, "All men are born carpenters, it's just some get waylaid along the way." I may not have been waylaid, but the "build it-fix it" gene surely was not passed down to me by my father. A broken lawn mower pull cord might as well have been a Cray supercomputer.

He knew how to operate the television tube tester at Snyder's Drug, and one time he helped me get my bike chain back on, but the list of his home improvement accomplishments makes for quick reading.

Yet I persisted; when I was six my favorite toy was a box of scrap lumber given to me by our neighbors, Donald and Effie Duck (real names, I swear). At eight I built a tree house in the backyard with lumber from our garage; all was fine until I overheard my father ask my mother, "Got any idea where the leaves to Mom's and Pop's dining room table went?"

In junior high I built skateboards using my sisters' roller skates for propulsion. Even in college I built a hut out of branches along a wooded stretch of the Minnesota River using only a pocketknife. Not all early projects were successes. When I was ten, I built a hutch for my sister's rabbit, Eloise. When we looked outside a few minutes after inducting Eloise into her pen, she was sitting on top of the hutch. She made a beeline for a nearby golf course and consumed an inordinate amount of crabgrass killer, and there was little need for the hutch after that.

I've built or radically remodeled every house I've owned. As a tradesperson I've worked on geodesic domes, earth-sheltered homes, barrel vault homes, historic houses, and everything in between. You name it, I've remodeled it. I love the tangibility of it all. I'm not necessarily a gifted carpenter, but I believe I'm — as Hot Lips Houlihan once told Major Burns in a fit of passion on an episode of *MASH* — "so . . . so . . . so above average." There are finish carpenters more meticulous and framing carpenters that are faster, but all in all I'm pretty damn good. And while I'm not a perfectionist, I am a completionist. And that counts for something.

Two qualities define successful tradespeople. First, they need to have the skills to do the job right. They need to know the techniques, materials, and tools, and how the three work together. A good plumber knows the rhythm and sizzle of a well-sweated copper joint. A good framing carpenter can drive 16d nails all day with a tap and two confident whacks. A seasoned drywall taper, waltzing on stilts, can apply three perfect coats of compound in the time it takes an amateur to get the lid off the five-gallon drywall bucket. Get the wrong tradesperson, and the concrete dips, the heat ducts pop, the floors squeak.

The second quality of good tradespeople is, oddly enough, knowing when good is good enough. They know the tolerances of their trade. They know when not to be unnecessarily precise, and unnecessarily expensive, and unnecessarily slow. A stud used for framing a door can be a quarter inch off the mark, but the trim around that door better be dead on. The grout line between handmade Mexican floor tiles can run fat and skinny, but the grout line between precision-cut Carrara marble tiles better be laser perfect. So knowing the tolerances is important. Tradespeople that are skilled and know the tolerances work in "the sweet spot." They're the ones you want to hire. They work efficiently. They have a reassuring confidence and pace.

Somewhere in the "Cabin Genre Writer's Guidelines" there's a clause that permits the author to mount his soapbox OPB (once per book) and get preachy about something. Sooo . . .

Red Green once said, "Using a hammer is easy. You just pick it up and keep hitting stuff until you've built something." While it's not that easy, most people — if they put their mind and bicep to it — can tackle parts of a building project; whether it's a cabin or a cabinet. People tend to be naturals at certain tasks. Engineers seem to get the whole electrical wiring thing; math lovers are often good at figuring out stair jacks and roof rafters; artists make good trim carpenters. I say, think about your gift; then get some skin in the game. Doing some of the work gives you bragging rights, adds to the mythical bank account, builds confidence, gives you more control over the schedule, and makes you popular, especially among your kids who have just bought houses. As a bonus, when you put something together, you know how to take it apart when something goes wrong.

There are roadblocks to DIYing. Certain trades carry a mystique about them, a mystique that, in some cases, dates back to the medieval guilds formed to protect the secrets of the craft. Don't let the mystique bamboozle. If you feel like biting off part of a project, at least give it a look. Learn the basics, get the lay of the land; the information is there for the plucking. Should you pour your own concrete foundation? No. Can you shingle a roof? Yes. Can you build your own cabin? At least part of it.

To learn the basics of a craft, go to lots of sources. Watch some YouTube videos; ask the guy down the block or in the next pew who does it for a living, "Hey, I'm gonna _____ this weekend. What are three things I should know?" Tackle a miniversion of a project before you tackle the maxi. Don't be afraid to make mistakes — all are fixable. Flip through home improvement books, magazines, and television shows — they're great sources of know-how. Take the information with a grain of salt; lots of DIY information is written by middle-aged men, sitting behind cluttered desks with exactly two pages or twenty-three minutes of airtime to teach you something. I know — I used to be one of them. Building does not take place in a plumb, level, and perfect world.

So let's say you decide to hang drywall. Not a bad choice; it's cheap, it doesn't leak, it can't shock you, and it can be cut with a three-dollar utility knife. But here's what happens if you tackle the job unenlightened: You cut the drywall too "loose" so there are big gaps and cracks in the corners, around outlets, and between sheets. Then you — or whoever is taping it — have to spend an extra weekend (when you could have been kayaking) filling gaps with drywall tape, mud, and patches. And it still might not look right.

But maybe you cut the drywall to fit too tight — so when you install the stuff you're bending and banging it to fit. You're busting off corners, cracking edges, cussing a little. Making it fit that tight isn't saving you work, it's creating more work. You should have taken the Goldilocks approach — not too tight, not too loose, but just right. And that's where a little know-how goes a long way.

Part of the problem with building materials like drywall, 2×4s, and plywood is, unlike everything else in the world, they don't come with a three-pound manual. You need to get yourself some learnin'.

And in closing, ladies and gentlemen, I will add this: when looking into the feasibility of doing a project, get a feel for the learning curve. If the curve is as steep as K2 — and you'll only do it once in your lifetime — maybe don't climb it. I refuse to install garage door openers, garbage disposals, and range hoods. They all involve skinned knuckles, lots of moving parts, and strange body contortions. It could take me days to learn the tricks of the trade, which I'll never use again. That's when I PAP (point and pay) instead of DIY.

Kat's and my intent is to do every lick of the project that involves nails, screws, or staples. We lay initial claim to the rough framing, siding, decks, roofing, windows, insulating, drywall, flooring, trim, and cabinets. These tasks rest firmly in our comfort zone. Nails and wood are things comprehensible; they're logical. Mistakes can be quickly remedied by yanking, unscrewing, or prying.

Plumbing and electricity are tasks we can legally tackle, *but* right now they're a little too K2-ish. They're not mountains we have the time to climb right now. We start nosing around to find the local tradespeople who work in the sweet spot.

We hear good things about an electrician named Justin, an escaped union tradesman from Minneapolis. He stops out when the rough frame of the cabin is complete, and we talk. He's really young; while we chat I swear his voice is changing. But he's confident yet laid back and drives a nice truck with a sign on it (not magnetic), which means he has a real business.

He's meticulous in his note taking and asks lots of questions. Since I want to do some of the bull work, he's fine working by the hour, rather than by the bid. We walk around and realize the cabin is so small there's no place to put the circuit panel inside. Outside is the only choice, not necessarily convenient when a breaker trips. Dinky also means putting the bathroom light switch outside the bathroom rather than in it. He has time in three weeks, so we shake.

The electrical part of the project is one we need to get legally and officially inspected. It's a state, not a local, mandate. So we go by the book. There's a "rough in" inspection when the inspector will check the raw, uncovered work. He'll make sure the proper size wires have been run; 14-gauge wires to bedrooms and living room, heftier 12-gauge wires to kitchen and bathroom (to accommodate power-sucking hair dryers and waffle irons). He'll make certain that wires running through holes less than 1¼ inches back from the face of a stud are covered by metal plates to protect them from nails and screws. He'll make sure certain things — such as microwaves, garbage disposals, and refrigerators — each have their own dedicated circuit to minimize overloads. He'll make sure of lots of things.

TEN ELECTRICAL THINGS YOU SHOULD KNOW — AND WHY
(WHETHER YOU DO THE WORK OR NOT)

1. **Outlets in living spaces can't be more than 12 feet apart, and there must be one within 6 feet of a corner.**

   WHY: Most lamps, portable heaters, and so on have 6-foot-long cords; this minimizes the temptation to use wimpy extension cords or to run them under throw rugs or through doorways.

2. **Outlets along kitchen counters can't be spaced more than 4 feet apart.**

   WHY: So people don't do moronic things like running appliance cords across the sink or plugging their waffle iron, coffeemaker, and juicer into a triple-outlet adapter.

3. **Kitchen lighting must be on a separate circuit from appliance outlets.**

   WHY: If your espresso machine trips a breaker, you won't be left in the dark while taking your turkey out of the oven.

4. **Any receptacle within 6 feet of a sink must be GFCI protected.**

   WHY: GFCI outlets minimize the chance of getting shocked. It's hard to reach more than 6 feet.

5. **In closets your light fixture has to be at least 6 inches (sometimes 12) from the edge of your top shelf.**

   WHY: So the clothes piled on the shelf can't catch on fire.

6. **Boxes for ceiling fans have to be specifically rated and correctly mounted.**

   WHY: You don't want a ceiling fan falling on you while you're asleep (or awake for that matter).

7. **Your bathroom outlet needs to be GFCI protected and on its own circuit.**

   WHY: Hair dryers trip breakers and fall into the bathtub all the time.

8. **Stairways with more than six steps need a light switch at both the top and the bottom.**

   WHY: So you don't break your neck in the dark.

9. **There has to be a hard-wired smoke detector within, or just outside, every bedroom, and all the detectors have to be wired together.**

WHY: (a) People forget to change batteries, and (b) if there's a fire, all the detectors go off to warn everyone in the house.

10. **Electrical boxes need to be sized based on the size and number of wires, wire nuts, and device going into them.**

    WHY: So boxes aren't crammed so full of stuff that shorts can occur.

NOTE: Codes change all the time, so check for updates.

Before Justin arrives, we nail up the boxes for switches, lights, and outlets so they're located where we want them. We also run Cat-5 wire to handle any future Internet, phone, or telecommunication technology. We're still debating the whole "to Internet or not to Internet thing," but it's no harder installing Cat-5 wire than standard telephone wire. Justin does all the rough wiring while Kat and I are in the city. It passes inspection.

When Justin comes to install the circuit breakers, switches, outlets, and lights, he brings his apprentice-wife. Kat is up working, and the four of us spend an afternoon BS-ing away while working. We find common ground in our fondness for kids, hiking, and Hawaii.

Halfway through the afternoon we hear an electrically charged *yelp* from the area where his wife is working. A few minutes prior to this I'd overheard Justin tell her he "thinks" the circuit she's working on is off. Many electricians harbor little fear of installing switches and outlets on a hot circuit; they're just very careful not to touch certain combinations of wires simultaneously. To further insulate themselves from harm when working with live wires, electricians sometimes work "one hand in pocket," so any stray current will complete its circuit down the side of the body, rather than from hand to hand; that is, through the heart. (Note: This is cocktail chatter, not a recommendation.) His wife's shock isn't a heart stopper, but it's one that brings a fair amount of adrenaline, cursing and, eventually, ribbing. They finish the job — still married.

I begin feeling off balance, crabby, and irritable during this part of the project. The barometer of this is my stormy "don't try to control me" attitude, which Kat reads like a meteorologist. She prods me toward one doctor for an antidepressant check and another for a physical. They up my Wellbutrin dosage, draw enough blood to fill a caulk gun, and run urine tests. I'm working on siding details when my cell phone rings. Dr. Gonzalez begins with the good news: My good and bad cholesterol are within the normal range, and this and that — but my mind is drifting; he seems to be warming up for some bad news.

He explains that my PSA count is high, which can mean three things. Again he starts with the minor things, so maybe something major is coming. I may have an infection. I may have an enlarged prostate; happens to lots of guys, but usually a little older. "Or it could be cancer." My shoulder blades melt. Cancer?

Where's the closest ER? How will I get the ceiling fan hung and flooring laid with tubes and chemo running through me? Where is my last will and testament? And when I ask him about the next crucial step, he tells me to come back in eight to twelve weeks.

"In eight to twelve weeks?"

"Yes, in eight to twelve weeks, to see if the PSA count is higher." He tells me to watch for three symptoms: trouble "getting the stream going," low flow, and frequent urination. The second I hang up I have to pee. Fifteen minutes later I pee again. Then in another fifteen. The cancer is surely raging. I feel a swelling between my groin and buns — the place I imagine a prostate would be located, but I'm not actually sure where or what a prostate actually is. And yes, that stream did look a little wimpy. I am a marked man.

Then I picture myself on the cabin window seat fading away. Peacefully viewing the moonrise over Superior — amid the uncovered fiberglass insulation and bare wires and unboxed tile . . . damn, I've got a job to finish here. I get biopsied, prodded, and tested more, and eventually my PSA count goes down, and I live to whap another staple in the vapor barrier.

———

We hire a plumber who ultimately gets the job done, but "ultimately" takes a long time. Easygoing is a nice character trait but doesn't bode well when you need the job done. Plumbing is the last "in the wall" task, and it's creating a roadblock to installing the insulation and drywall.

Part of the problem is the plumber is a 73-by-23-inch man doing work in a 42-inch crawl space with a 24-by-24-inch trapdoor. He starts the job, then disappears. I walk in the door after being gone two weeks — two weeks in which he's promised to finish the job — and am so pleased to find he's left the place spotless. In fact, it looks as clean as when we left; almost like he'd never been there. He'd never been there. Like doctors, plumbers occasionally need to tend to emergencies, but we start feeling like the doctor is permanently out.

It's not like we're plumbing a water park here. There are kitchen and bathroom sinks, the shower, the toilet, the washing machine, and an outside faucet, all within 10 feet of each other. Installing the hot- and cold-water supply lines is by far the easiest part. Since they're under pressure, water will run through them regardless of the twists and turns; you could run them in figure eights if you wanted. You just don't want them to freeze.

But the drain-waste-vent (DWV) system is complicated. The drainpipes need to slope toward the septic at the correct angle; that slope being about ¼ inch per foot. Too steep and the liquids drain too fast to push the solids along; too gradual and nothing will drain at all. The DWV pipes are big — up to 4 inches in diameter — so big, most bathrooms have at least one 2×6 wall to accommodate their largeness. To complicate the equation every fixture must be vented vertically through the roof. The vents allow the water to drain freely without gurgling. (Picture how water won't drain out of a straw with your finger capping one end; but move it just a hair to create a "vent," and it flows freely.) The vents also carry odors and gases up and out of the house. There's more to plumbing than "poop runs downhill."

Our plumber sheepishly appears while I'm fiddling away on odds and ends the next Saturday. I'm in slow-burn mode. When he asks how I'm doing I respond "waterless." I try tormenting him by playing *The Blues Hour* full tilt because he's clearly a country-western guy. It doesn't faze him. Most plumbers I know are a bit thick-skinned to begin with, the recipients of oodles of crap on the job site. (See "poop runs downhill" above.) Plus they need to agonize through "the mushroom effect," a phenomenon in which seemingly small problems mushroom into colossal ones — especially in old houses. It usually plays out like this: There's a little drip under the sink. The plumber tightens a nut on the P-trap, and the thing disintegrates. He begins to install a new P-trap, but the pipe coming out of the wall is some old, archaic dimension. He finds an adapter, and as he's putting it on, that pipe breaks — inside the wall. He opens up the wall to fix that pipe and discovers rotten wall studs. And a small empire of silverfish. And . . .

But we're not dealing with the "mushroom effect," we're dealing with the "snail effect." I begin working on a monologue that extols the virtues of taking "the road less traveled" — *unless that road is the one leading to our cabin, and the one doing the traveling is a plumber.* And just as I'm about to mount the podium I realize the guy in the crawl space is holding some serious cards that could hold up progress for weeks if he chooses to play them that way. So within an hour we're chatting and downing Cokes. He finishes.

Getting water to the cabin is Panama Canal-ish in its complexity. It involves digging a 5-foot-deep trench from the lake, up the steep hillside, to the cabin. It involves installing 1-inch tubing to carry the water and an underground electric cable to carry power to the pump.

It requires the plumber to install the pressure tank, a small reservoir tank inside the cabin that signals the pump to push more water up. It takes the electrician wiring the pump and pressure tank. It requires the installation of a sediment filter and three trumpet-size water filter cartridges, each with progressively finer filters. It becomes impossible to imagine all of these elements working in harmony to produce that thing we take so for granted — water.

Finally, everything is in place. We flick a switch and stare at the end of a hose we've rigged up. The hose flinches, we hear a gurgle, see a trickle, then out comes a gush of cold pure water. Damn, Ma, we's hit a gusher. Oma Tupa is baptized.

TEN PLUMBING THINGS YOU SHOULD KNOW — AND WHY
(WHETHER YOU DO THE WORK OR NOT)

1. Find the main shut-off valve to your house, label it with a big tag and show everyone in your family where it is.

    WHY: If there's a leak, burst pipe, busted faucet, or some other emergency, someone can at least turn off the water to the whole house until you figure out the problem.

2. Install your PVC drain-waste-and-vent (DWC) pipes before you install your hot and cold water pipes and electrical wiring.

    WHY: Your DWV pipes are large and need to be strategically installed in order for the drains to drain and vents to vent properly. Run your hot and cold water pipes and wiring later; they're smaller and easily routed as needed.

3. If possible, locate your bathrooms, laundry room, and kitchen in a centralized area (or stacked atop one another).

    WHY: You'll use less material and labor for the initial installation, and subsequent maintenance will also be easier.

Plumbing "cores" also make it easier to winterize and "unwinterize" your cabin.

4. **Drainage pipes should slope between 1/8 inch and 1/4 inch per foot.**

   WHY: Too much slope, and the water will drain too fast without carrying away the waste; too little slope, and water won't have enough *oomph* to carry anything away.

5. **Use PEX plastic pipe for new or replacement hot and cold water pipe.**

   WHY: It's more DIY friendly than copper; some systems go together by crimping (versus soldering). If your cabin freezes, pipes are less likely to burst.

6. **Get to know and love your septic system — then treat it with respect.**

   WHY: A properly built and maintained septic system can last forty years or more; a poorly maintained one can fail in a few years. Minimize (or eliminate) garbage disposal use. Avoid disposing of oils, coffee grounds, pharmaceuticals, paint, paint thinners, and grease in your septic system. Have the tank pumped every few years.

7. **Be paranoid about winter.**

   WHY: Frozen water exerts a tremendous amount of pressure and can crack toilets, pipes, P-traps, your nerves, etc. (See chapter 15.) Install a freeze alarm. (See chapter 15.) Learn how to program the freeze alarm. (See chapter 15.)

8. **Use Teflon tape when installing any kind of threaded pipe.**

   WHY: It helps "lubricate" the pipes so they go together easier, helps seal threads to prevent leaks, and makes fitting easier to take apart later. A two-dollar roll will last you approximately a lifetime.

9. **Use your digital camera or phone to take a "before" photo of your plumbing if you're doing a repair or replacing something.**

WHY: When you go to the hardware store to buy new parts you won't have to spend thirty minutes trying to sketch things out for the salesperson — or sixty minutes making each return trip.

10. **Avoid tackling plumbing repairs on Sunday night.**

   WHY: Hardware stores are often closed. And if something goes wrong or the "mushroom effect" strikes, you may pay a plumber overtime or weekend rates to rescue you.

For heat we go with the quadruple-source approach. The Jøtul wood-stove will be the "go to" heat creator while we're at the cabin, and the skinny propane wall furnace will handle things while we're away. We put an electric toe kick heater in the kitchen and embed electric resistance heat beneath the bathroom tile floor. For the uninitiated — for those who have never stepped out of a shower, shivering on a cold day with wet hair, and had their feet land on a toasty warm floor — get initiated.

During the second winter I hang the drywall. The first area I tackle is the little alcove at the back of the cabin. The idea is to create a "clean room," one small area of sanity that's finished so we have at least one place to store clothes, food, and bodies away from the dust and construction chaos. I lie on my back like an upturned cockroach and use both legs and arms to hoist the 4-by-10 sheets onto the low part of the ceiling. I use little blocks of wood and boxes to hold it in place while screwing it to the ceiling rafters. I get 'er done, but when it comes to hanging the rest, I head to Julie's Hardware and rent their drywall lift; a device that let's you crank, rather than wrestle, sheets into position.

I hang all the rest of the drywall, and there's not a single full sheet. There are beams, outlets, and windows to cut around. There are angles at the roofline. Pros often charge by the square foot for hanging dry-wall, but any hanger would go bankrupt on this gig. I become bankrupt in a different way; I just plain old get sick of it. But there's an upside: again the cabin assumes a new look. The riot of yellow insulation, blue electrical boxes, copper pipe, and wood framework all disappear behind the simplicity of smooth gray drywall. The cabin looks smaller but feels way more cabin-ish.

To make a wall covered with a patchwork of 4-by-8 sheets of drywall look like one big flat surface, you need to "tape it." If it were only as easy as it sounds. At the seams between the sheets you trowel on a bed of drywall compound, then embed paper drywall tape. When this dries you cover the paper with progressively wider swaths of compound, allowing each coat to dry in between. You do the same at the corners. And at the ceiling. You dab all the screw holes with mud. In trompe l'oeil the artist attempts to "fool the eye" into seeing something that's not there. In drywall taping the taper attempts to fool the eye into not seeing something that is there.

Good tapers, like good tennis players, make it all look so easy. I serve nothing but net. When I break out the drywall trowel and start swathing on drywall compound, the results look like Jackson Pollock's *Convergence*.

After three days of slinging "mud" across the floor, the boom box, my forehead, and some drywall seams, I take inventory. I'm not having fun, a severe infraction of Rule #1. I'm spending plenty of time sanding in between coats. It ain't looking all that great. If taping looks bad, it doesn't matter how perfect your framing, painting, or trim work looks, you've blown it.

I once again find an ingenious way to get the job done fast. I call a local taper. We never see or meet him. Everything – introduction, bid, questions, progress reports – is conducted via phone. When we're up on weekends, he isn't around and vice versa. We meet his stilts, his mud-caked radio, his lunchbox, his mixing paddle, but not him. From his voice he sounds large and bearded, but he may look like Pee-wee Herman. He might *be* Pee-wee Herman. But it doesn't matter. He does a good job.

For about half the project I work alone; it confirms that the older I get, the less I enjoy the solitary life. When I was in college I could think of no grander adventure than to toss a raincoat, change of underwear, and pack of RyKrisp in my old Cub Scout backpack, stick my thumb out, grab a dumpy hotel room in some blue highway town, then ponder life and write. I could go seventy-two hours and utter fewer than fifty words, half of those to the spider in the bathtub.

But slowly my love of the hermit life has diminished. One day I was hiking in the woods and realized I hadn't been thinking profound or life-changing thoughts at all — I'd been counting footsteps and trying to remember the exact phrasing of old Crest toothpaste commercials. "Crest has been shown to be an effective decay preventive dentifrice when used in a conscientiously applied program of . . . of . . ." Well, did it say "significant value"? Or did it go right into that part about oral hygiene?

After working alone for days on end, my social, parental, and spousal skills get sluggish. When I arrive home I'm still on North Shore time, out of touch with Kat's and the kid's lives, behind at work, and a little bit owly. Kat and I develop a system for ratcheting this down. For my part I admit — out loud — "I feel a little bit crabby." And Kat's part is to say, "It's okay to be a little bit crabby." This simple exchange makes me only half as crabby.

Another downside to working alone is there is no one to tell you when to quit, no one to point out you look like the subject of an Edvard Munch painting. This not-recognizing-when-to-quit becomes manifest one late afternoon.

I'm having a "bad carpentry day" so decide to put the hammer down and install the outside lights. I can't quite reach the wires, so I kick aside a pile of scraps and drag my legless table saw over as a step stool. Still a little short, I stack 2×6s on that. I still have to stretch to reach the wires, but I'll be damned if I'm going to waste 60 seconds moving a stepladder 8 feet over. That would be stupid. I'm stretching and cranking on the wire nuts when the table saw tips. The Mousetrap Game begins. The light fixture hits the deck as I fall sideways. I become the gravitational force for a catapult of scrap lumber launching a five-pound box of shingle nails into the air. I catch my balance and plant a foot solidly in the middle of a pack of light bulbs, then reel backward and step on one of the shingle nails, point up. Blood is a good indicator that it must be quittin' time.

Tales of bizarre accidents are a popular topic on the job site. There's the carpenter who bumps into the nail gun his partner is carrying and takes a 16d nail through the skull. There's the guy who welds his wedding ring to an I-beam in the basement and has to wait until morning for someone to cut him loose.

It's not easy to separate urban legend from urban truth. One oft-repeated story involves a carpenter working on a high rise in Chicago when a gust of wind catches the plywood he's carrying, and depending on the version, he either hang glides into Soldier Field or is found floating in Lake Michigan. Even more oft repeated is the tale of the painter who cleans his brush out over the toilet, cops a squat, has a smoke, tosses his cigarette butt in the toilet, and when the paint thinner explodes he scorches the boys. The ambulance guys carrying him hear the story and laugh so hard they drop the stretcher, and the guy winds up with a broken arm to boot.

One of my jobs at *Family Handyman* magazine was sorting through the submissions for the Great Goofs column, the most popular department in the magazine. The acts of goofiness were legion: people drywalling cats into their ceilings; mechanics air-ratcheting nuts onto their fingers; guys setting ladders in pickup beds to extend their reach, then having their wife drive off. One guy — sitting on the john reading superglue instructions — glued his elbows to his knees, couldn't get his pants up, and his wife had to drive him to the ER with a garbage bag wrapped around his lower half.

To offset the dangers on the job site, there's plenty of jostling and ribbing. When you screw up a measurement, you bark, "I cut it twice and it's still too short." When you bend a nail you yelp, "Must-a pulled that one outta the bent nail box." When you whack yourself on the thumb, you curse, "Hit the wrong #@?!# nail." When you gotta take a whiz you announce, "Going out back to take a perc test."

But through the highs and lows, the chuckles and splinters, the sore muscles, and the glorious spring days, it's all worth it, because soon we'll have a cabin — and we have plenty of kids to fill it.

XIII

FAMILY
MATTERS

Life is a fluid, not a solid. It changes.
Be ready for it.

BLENDING A FAMILY OF FOUR TEENAGERS, a nine-year-old, a territorial Pekingese, a forty-year-old ex-hippie and a thirty-four-year-old, high-energy saleswoman was a white-water rafting trip without the guide, maps, or life jackets. Things looked so calm when we launched the raft, "Oh, baby, look at the scenery! The sun is shining! This is the life!"

But "Hmm, what's up around that bend? Geez, this calm little stream can't turn into a wild river this fast, can it?" And then we saw it. Churning and rapids everywhere. Kat and I steered like mad to direct the raft to calmer waters, but we kept darting into raging whirlpool after raging whirlpool. We tied ourselves in, duct-taped ourselves to the rudder. We had forgotten to read *The Art of Hassle-Free Family Blending,* and the time to read it wasn't when we were about to capsize.

We had kids skipping school, smoking, shoplifting, doing things you shouldn't do until you're twenty-one, and even then you shouldn't be doing them. We got to know teachers, neighbors, police, and counselors on a first-name basis. Two of our daughters engaged in a "Who can find the sleaziest boyfriend" contest. They both won. Just as we thought we'd made it through the class 4 rapids, the class 5 rapids appeared. Holidays were brutal — kids with pants the size of the *Hindenburg,* and my temper nearly as explosive.

Our blended family and marriage spun out of control for two years. In most blended families problems arise when the kids from each household can't get along. Our problem was our kids got along too well. Kat and I felt outnumbered. We all lived in a state of wince. Yet we Napoleonicly forged ahead, doing things as a family — because that's what families do. We'd pile everyone in the van and drive the 200 miles to Bemidji to visit Kat's mom. All the kids had CD players with headphones cranked up to chain-saw level, with a cacophony of rap, heavy metal, and country music. There wasn't much parent-child interaction those days except "I need more batteries!" At restaurants I'd imagine people whispering, "Isn't it nice of that couple to take those kids from the juvenile detention center out for lunch?" There were plenty of stretches of calm water along the way, plenty of victories, lots of laughter — but there were plenty of hazards lurking just below the surface.

The term *stepfamily* has all but disappeared from the American vocabulary; Cinderella, with a stepmother who locked her in the closet and two stepsisters mean as fungus, didn't help endear the term to anyone. So *blended family* has become the vanguard term.

Family therapist Ron Deal doesn't think *blended* is the singular best culinary metaphor. He suggests some families are "pressure cooked," where values, traditions, and preferences are forced together under pressure to create a single homogenous dish (at the risk of blowing the top off the pot).

Some families are "tossed," where the values and traditions of each person and family are thrown into the air with the hopes they'll land in some form of perfect dish.

Some are microwaved, where the families try to become a "nuke-lier" family in a flash.

The kid painting crew, before the paint roller fights began

Deal's recommendation is to use the "Crock-Pot style," where the individual ingredients remain intact, but the juices slowly flow together under low, consistent heat. That's what we tried to do — but it's awkward explaining to people you're a Crock-Pot family. Raising teenagers is a tug-of-war — one that can last years. Neither team is letting go of their side of the rope. Each team is trying to get the other one over the center mark; to see their point of view. There's a lot of seesawing back and forth. The rope gets stretched to its limit. You are exhausted. You find reserves you didn't know you had. You dig in your heels. But as a parent you never let go. Even when night falls you keep the tension on the rope because the other team — regardless of what they do or say — need to know you're there.

And if all goes well, eventually, both sides put down the rope, hug, and celebrate, because it was a battle well fought. No one lost any fingers. Both teams are stronger for what they've gone through. It's worth it — you just gotta rub a lot of rosin on your hands and hold on tight.

We never gave up on our kids or each other or this family we were trying to Crock-Pot together. We marinated our kids in love. We worked. We talked. We sought professional help. We survived, eventually thrived. It's almost impossible to look at our children now — calmly wielding paintbrushes, mature, alive, laughing — and believe they are the same people. I'm sure they look at us and think the same. We're not only blended, we're blessed. We'll never intermingle DNA, but we've intermingled our lives. Now our highest highs come from just being together.

Our intent is to create a family cabin — a retreat to remain in the family for generations. A place with notches on the edge of a door to measure heights summer by summer, fish tales that grow, old wool jackets with petrified sticks of gum in the pocket, funny-shaped rocks on the mantel, standing jokes, cribbage boards with one missing peg. People, children, jobs, and houses may come and go, but we want this cabin to remain a constant.

Our intent, too, is for our kids to take part in the blisters and sawdust of building. Work — so they will feel a part of the cabin and its history. Work — so they can see that this isn't something that just appears on the shores of Lake Superior, full-blown like Hera from Zeus's head. Work — so we can spend time together as a family. Work — to learn skills. Work — to get the thing done. And work they do. And do so joyfully. Usually.

Once the rough framework is up, we begin having more and more work weekends. Sometimes all five kids converge; other times just one or two. Some weekends the older two camp at nearby Tettegouche campgrounds with boyfriends. Other times we all camp out on the floor of the unfinished cabin or stay at the Mariner Motel. Cuisine ranges from Subway sandwiches spiced with sawdust to simple meals at greasy spoons that taste like banquets.

Initially they do the standard kid-work: paint, haul stuff, and clean up. They prime and paint siding, scrap out the cabin, clear brush and burn the remains. But the more the kids work, the more they prove they're capable of skilled labor. Kellie and I lay the tongue-and-groove floor. Maggie drills the beams, installs the metal support brackets, then bolts everything together. Zach drills the vent holes in the eave blocking with a mammoth right-angle drill — the kind that will wrench your arm off if it hits a knot — and installs the vents. Tessa caulks around the windows and rafters. Sarah installs cedar decking. Kids cut and fit the Tyvek house wrap, nail windows in place, split firewood, insulate.

Friends and boyfriends pitch in, too. One weekend Sarah paints a large blue heart on the wall with her and her boyfriend's initials inside. The next weekend she rollers him out after they break up.

We work at the cabin in various combinations and numbers; sometimes in sevens, other times twos. One night while two-ing it, Tessa and I lie on our backs on the deck on a moonless night, a billion stars punched through the black blanket of sky. The conversation comfortably meanders here and there. She's the youngest but was pulled ahead in years by the adolescent vortex of four older siblings. Between that and the divorce, a couple of years of her childhood got dissolved in the fizz. When you're nine and need to pick your way through the flotsam of divorce, you put order in your life wherever you can. That's hung with Tessa. She is a kid of meticulousness and perfection.

I've spent plenty of time forehead-slapping myself and rehashing how I could have done things better through the separation and divorce. But the "Give up all hope of creating a happier past" saying is truth. So we work on creating a happier now. Right now we've got it.

The first casualty of divorce is your children's past. They had a life before the split; there were family trips, funny things said and done, stories of childbirth, goofy first words, memorable first steps. But in order to survive a divorce, to keep the painful parts at bay, the tendency — as an adult — is to *not* bring up *any* part of the past, even the good parts. Maybe you're with family and friends and someone talks about the time Willy put a worm in Trisha's SpaghettiOs, and one of your kids did something equally goofy, but you keep hushed. Because it was back *then*. And if it was good back then, what happened to make it not good? And in staying hushed, you've robbed your children of their history; of the stories and experiences that made them, them. Unhushing the hush is hard, but Kat and I keep getting better at this each year. Our children deserve a past.

Many are the weeks without children. There are stretches when I spend so many weekends away I feel like Deadbeat Dad; my natural tendency is to point north every chance I've got. Kat picks up the slack, and five kids create a lot of slack.

Midway through the first full year of construction, Kat and I discover something about our parenting dynamics. Whenever she's out of town, working on the cabin or dogsledding or sailing, and I'm single parenting, family life feels subdued and lifeless. Without Kat's energy things feel out of balance; all of my opaque parenting weaknesses turn transparent. Things don't feel as fun and full. And I'm a terrible housekeeper. I've been banned from the laundry room since I soaked a pair of Maggie's stained jeans in straight bleach overnight, threw them in the dryer, then opened the door to discover only a zipper, one pocket, and two handfuls of lint.

Without Kat I'm more withdrawn, more likely to spend the evening reading in our bedroom than sitting on the kitchen floor with a bowl of ice cream discussing friends. Things just feel duddy.

And then she reveals that when I'm away she feels the family runs flat. She thinks I'm the spirit maker, the life of the party, the one who keeps things light and in perspective. And it becomes clear that it requires both of us to create a three-dimensional home. I'm the comedian, she's the counselor. I'm the homework go-to guy, Kat's the accountant and appointment maker. The kids will talk to her about anything — and when the conversation gets too heavy, I'll drag it out of the abyss. When you average out Kat's tendency to worry and my tendency to not worry, fretting finds a balance.

In mid-July of the second summer of building, we head to the cabin with eighty percent of our kids. We're determined to have a weekend consisting of no more than fifty percent work, with the rest play. We stick ninety percent to our game plan.

That night the cabin actually starts feeling like a cabin — unfinished, yet comfortable. There's water and electricity. We simply hang out. We are the only animals on the ark; the rest of the world has disappeared. There's no place to go and no incoming digital signals. The phone has a "don't touch me unless you're dialing 911" aura. There are no forms of entertainment except one another. It is a blessing, a slowing down. We play games like Pit and a family favorite called Screw Your Neighbor. We play cribbage and drink gallons of soda. Bowlsful of chips disappear. It's a slow waltz. We reminisce, cook, read, color, do crossword puzzles, talk. Maggie is learning the guitar, and we fiddle with that.

I lie on the floor amidst my wife and four daughters — Zach is working as a landscaper in Maryland for the summer — and think I should write a book called *Alone in the House of Estrogen*. Or as Michael Perry, who lives in an equally gender-imbalanced household, writes, "I don't have a family, I have a sorority." Yet I don't feel awkward, uncomfortable, or outnumbered. I feel happy.

The kids roll their sleeping bags out in the little loft of the bump-out, and the slumber party chatter slowly diminishes as they drift off one by one. Life is good.

Even Katie, our old Pekingese, enjoys herself. At home we need to keep her on a chain or walk her on a leash, since her natural tendency is to go in search of the nearby bed-and-breakfast where the house-keeper once fed her an entire ham sandwich. But at the cabin she can wander freely. There's no way her bowed 4-inch legs can propel her up the steep, rocky driveway onto the hazards of Highway 61. She seems utterly content sniffing around for long-departed deer. And the cabin, sizewise, is more to her scale.

———

One evening later that summer we get a call from Zach that begins with the words no parent wants to hear: "Now I'm going to tell you something, but *don't* panic." It is in the brief instant between this sentence and the next that imagination breaks the sound barrier. He's in jail, in the hospital, in treatment, in the army now; he's tattooed a swastika on his forehead while drunk; impregnated one, two, three girls; become a Moonie; been voted president of the Jeffrey Dahmer fan club.

And then the next sentence comes, "I hurt myself at work . . ."

The imagination shifts to the world of grisly accidents. He's blind, paralyzed, his entire arm caught in a leaf shredder.

". . . with a chain saw."

Lord of terrors, he's limbless, full of Frankenstein scars, on life support, he's dialed our phone number with a pencil clenched between shattered teeth!

"But, really, I'm okay."

"Well, just how okay are you?"

He's twenty-six-stitches-across-the-knee okay. At the end of a long day clearing a hillside, he'd swung his arm down to rest and the chain caught his pants, then knee, then skin, then tissue. He's out of work for two weeks. He's much calmer than either Kat or me. With a light heart he says, "Hey, Daddy-o, now I look even *more* like you."

———————

If I were to write a book on parenting, it would be short. But somewhere in the first two pages I'd throw out the idea that the best way to connect with a kid — even one approaching Pluto's orbit or pacing dents in the floor — is to get away one on one. Not the five-minute, "I need to talk to you in the corner" one on one, but the road-trip kind. No lectures and no agenda. When Zach launched into his calamitous adolescent years — and he was a prodigy at it — we started a tradition of heading to the Boundary Waters to camp and canoe for four or five days. It was just Zach, the black flies, SPAM, and me. The wilderness created a level playing field. We each had a paddle, half a canoe, a pack, and, all too frequently, no idea where we were.

And within that tradition, another tradition was born. He was thirteen. We were sitting on the edge of a lake after a full day of canoeing, and I pulled a couple of cigars from my pack. He went gosh-eyed. We fired them up and decreed any topic was fair game while we puffed. It was man to man. We could talk about women and girls, work and school, secrets, family, friends. No judging, no lectures. What happened on the Gunflint stayed on the Gunflint. Sometimes, even now, even in the big city, even when he's legal, we have a cigar when life gets hard.

———————

Maybe I started the cigar tradition early, because I never got to it with my father. Pa got up one Saturday morning thinking it was pretty much like any other day, headed out for his weekly game of tennis, and died of a massive heart attack. There are worse ways to go than surrounded by friends you've known for thirty years, doing something you love. But better yet, it would have been better not to die so young.

At fifty-eight, Pa was heading for retirement. One of his goals was to move to the cabin he and my mother had bought in Waverly, hang out his shingle, and run for mayor. There was nothing grandiose about the dream or the dreamer — but you could see the arc in his eye when he talked about it.

I never got to say goodbye to Pa. In fact, on an adult level I never really got to say hello. There's a point in a father-son relationship when it shifts from being an adult-child bond and becomes an adult-adult one. It's when the faucet that pours out wisdom about marriage, child-rearing, finances, and how to live life is cranked open. And you know that water is safe and pure; it can come from no other source. But I'd been absent. I'd spent five years wading through college, two years teaching in Denver, then moved to the Ozarks in a failed attempt to move back to the land. My time with him had been limited to a quick visit here and there. The faucet had never been turned on.

We were within pitching-wedge distance of having that man-to-man conversation; the ball was heading straight for the hole when it took the worst imaginable bounce and landed in the worst imaginable hazard. Maggie had just been born, and my folks were a day or two away from driving down to the Ozarks to spend a few days. Here is where it would happen — a couple of lawn chairs overlooking Bull Shoals, a couple of cigars, and some "I wanna give you a little piece of advice about that." But when the neighbors drove up to tell us which day Ma and Pa were arriving (we were without telephone), instead of saying "Wednesday," they said, "Your father died this morning." Not having had that conversation with Pa is a regret I carry in my pocket like a sharp stone. I wish I could have cupped my hands under that faucet to take a few deep, long drinks. Had a few puffs on that cigar.

I learned plenty about life from watching the way Pa lived, and a little more after he died. We found a "Code of Life" scrawled on a piece of paper tucked in the back of his desk drawer. It read:

- Let me achieve and hold fast to:
- An awareness that my problems and successes are gnatlike in another's eyes.
- Simplification. The will to do it now.
- Seeing the best in others and ignoring idle criticism about them.
- Honesty with others, even though I may deceive myself. Never taking myself seriously, but only my job.
- Some personal privacy and respect for the same in others.
- Recognition of substance from trivia and fighting only for the former.
- The ability to laugh with others.
- A few friends who share these views.

I think, "What better place to rehearse these ideals than the cabin? What better place to practice them than in real life?"

———————

At one point during the project, we take our annual elder-family retreat to Halcyon Harbor, the elder family being my two sisters and their spouses, my mother and her husband Frank, Kat and me. Halcyon is a quirky fairyland resort perched — literally — above Lake Superior. The most notorious cabin is the "Cliff House," which is cantilevered over Superior on mammoth iron beams. If you cut a hole in the screen-porch floor you could fish for salmon below. You could never, ever build a cabin like that today, but it's grandfathered in, and there it sits.

Two other cabins are an architect's nightmare of additions, alterations, and converging rooflines. The cabin we retreat to is the Lake House — the largest, most normal dwelling of the lot. Yet it is far from ordinary. It has twenty-five mirrors and a massive fieldstone fireplace.

The bathroom sports avocado fixtures with deco styling. The sink has a molded-in waterfall faucet and, though forty years old, could grace the pages of the most recent Kohler catalog. The toilet — for lack of a better analogy — has a Harley Davidson seat. It is the halfway place where Babe Ruth and Jack Dempsey drank themselves to sleep while sojourning to their Naniboujou Lodge north of Grand Marais.

Halcyon is the place where Kat and I would retreat early in our marriage when our lives were in need of mending. We always stayed at The Studio, a small nook nestled in the rafters of one of the larger units. It was here — with fireplace, wide-eyed view of Superior, birdfeeder plunked 3 feet from the picture window — we would retreat to knit our unraveling lives back together. It represented everything we didn't have — order, innocence, peace.

But Halcyon has a different aura on the elder-family retreat. Everyone is relaxed. Each couple is in charge of one meal, so no one feels overburdened. The screen porch provides the perfect hangout, since half the family smokes and the other half detests it. There is always a plate of smoked fish, caramel corn, or peanuts to munch. Frank wears grooves in the cribbage board. We play Yahtzee, Screw Your Neighbor, "The Dice Game," and Scrabble into the wee hours of the morning.

With no minors to influence badly, everyone is raunchier. On this particular weekend Kat and I spend a day working at the cabin before driving down to meet everyone at Halcyon. My mother recalls we were going to invite Dick and Jean over for breakfast at the cabin that morning and turns to Kat, asking, "Did you have Dick for breakfast?" My sisters pounce all over that. We howl, tears running down our faces. For the rest of the weekend, no meal can be eaten without reference to oral sex.

It's a slumber party for old folks. After Christmas, Thanksgiving, Easter, and other family get-togethers, everyone packs up after dinner and heads home. Here we linger, laugh, and lollygag. You get to know family in a different way.

While we're putting some belated finishing touches on the cabin, four of our kids head for college in a single week, scattering like balls from a Golfing 101 class.

I drive Maggie out to the University of Montana in Missoula, where she's transferred to finish her senior year in accounting. She likes the West, but I think she more likes the idea of escaping the blur of a blended family in search of some self-definition.

Maggie actually started life in a rustic cabin — a thing that, at the time, we called a house. It was in the middle of the Ozarks, small and built mostly with salvage material from an old Baptist church. There was no electricity, water, or phone, and the road was no more than a couple of passes of a dropped dozer blade. We didn't last long. Shortly after my father died, we moved back to Minnesota, partly to be with Ma, but partly because we were so ill-equipped to handle the back-to-the-land life.

She was a child born of strong confidence and full throttle, who developed some engine trouble in high school and is now regaining speed. It is this history that sits with us as her Nissan Sentra clicks past mile after mile of freeway, sunflower fields, and mountains. She's a young woman headed for adventure, yet still my child. It's not until we cross into Mountain Time that my heart dips a little. She reaches over and adjusts the clock from 10:04 to 9:04. We've never lived in different time zones.

Zach, Kellie, and Sarah head in radically different directions (La Crosse, Stevens Point, and Duluth) to pursue their radically different majors: English, interior design, and early childhood education. It's funny how they all head in such diverse directions on the vocational compass. But they're each passionate about their choice, and they each make it work in their own unique way.

Tessa becomes an only child, and Kat and I feel like empty nesters since she's a perpetual motion machine. She works, is in plays and choir, leads music for Sunday night youth services, has a boyfriend. And we realize, life changes; it's a fluid, not a solid. We need to be ready for it.

As kids strike out on their own, life feels a little hollow. Yet there are constant reminders of the goodness — like the night I was walking through the waterfront area of Philadelphia with Gary, editor in chief of the magazine where I work. We'd taped two television segments for a home improvement show that morning. We'd had an expense account dinner and solid conversation. We'd stopped at a tattoo parlor, where Gary had gotten a heart tattoo with a ribbon across it bearing his wife's name. As we neared our hotel Gary stopped, put his hand on my shoulder, and said, "Spike, shut your eyes, take a deep breath. We have full stomachs, meaningful work, and families that love us. Life doesn't get any better than this. Right here, right now." That was my tattoo for the night.

XIV

Finishing
TOUCHES

When it's ninety percent finished, it's finished.

I ONCE INTERVIEWED A WOMAN WHO, over the course of a forty-year career, had dreamt up over 10,000 names for paint. Included were "My Place or Yours," "The Ego Has Landed," and "What Inheritance?" — offbeat names, but when Pat Verlodt showed me the swatches, I realized she'd nailed 'em.

"A woman doesn't want to call her neighbor and tell her to run over to look at paint #8260," Pat explained. "She wants to tell her she's painted her kitchen 'Moon Goddess' or '3 a.m. Latte.' There's romance in a paint name."

But there's more than romance; there's psychology. And Pat gave me the Cliff's Notes version.

Yellow is a happy color. But an overly vibrant yellow can wear you down or stimulate feelings of frustration. "And some shades of yellow do not reflect well on humanity in the early morning," Pat added. Greens, associated with grass, trees, and nature, conjure up feelings of growth and vitality, yet are calming at the same time. Blues — the most beloved colors, but not the most popular paintwise — make people think about water, blue skies, and relaxing things. "But it's not a good kitchen color," Verlodt clarified. "It's so anti-appetite that some weight loss plans have their clients eat off blue plates."

Reds, on the other hand, can stimulate appetite and heart rate. Note the color in the logos of McDonald's, KFC, Dairy Queen, and Burger King. But it can be overstimulating; you can't live with red for long. The same red that draws you into a restaurant pushes you out quickly — fine for a fast-food joint but not for Oma Tupa.

Beiges — the best-selling paint colors of all — are conservative. They may not get your room into *Architectural Digest*, but they're livable and provide a nice backdrop for other colorful things.

"But there's no wrong color," Pat explained. "The best way to tell if you like a color is to live with it for a while." So that's what we do. The cabin is so wide open from top to bottom that we only get one shot at a color for the main space. And one for the bathroom — the only room with a door on it.

Kat's been reading articles by homeowners who have become down-right suicidal after painting a whole room a certain color based on what a 2-by-3-inch paint swatch looked like. She starts buying quarts and painting card table–size swatches on the walls. The colors change like a chameleon based on the time of day, the cloud cover, how many lights are on, even the kind of bulb in the fixture. We've already got a riot — or at least a small demonstration — of color going on: a bright blue stove, a Technicolor stained glass parrot window, zingy Fiestaware plates, woods of several hues, a bright orange couch on order. We start thinking the "beige backdrop" route.

———

We know we want wood paneling on the tall wall facing the lake; there's just something woodish about it. So one Saturday on the way to the cabin, daughter Sarah and I make a side trip to Aurora, Minnesota, home of Jim's Native Wood.

It gives us plenty of time to talk and reflect. Kat and I married and merged lives when Sarah was fifteen. Fifteen is hard enough without moving twenty miles and starting sophomore year at a new school.

Hard enough without inheriting one sister in the same grade, another sister six years younger, and a brother — a thing you'd never before had in your life, and surely not had in your house before. Hard enough when you already have one dad and this forty-two-year-old stranger with a Fu Manchu mustache and a basketball hoop in his kitchen suddenly gets Velcroed to your life and holds sway over what you do. It's not like it was a kidnapping; there were plenty of discussions. But when you're only fourteen percent of the vote and running the corn maze between childhood and adulthood, it sure adds some twists and turns to the course.

We fought our battles. We had our stare downs. Sarah was a tough kid. She played hockey, pitched softball, and knew how to replace brake linings before she could drive. We busted a few tie-rods on the road to figuring out who we were to each other. But the road's smoothed out. I love her as a daughter and, no small matter, like her as a person.

━━━━━

Jim's is a one-man show. He has a small sawmill, a small kiln for drying, and a small machine for planing and edging. His output is antlike by Boise Cascade standards, but while their wood is white bread, Jim's is a hearty whole wheat.

The smell of ash, birch, cedar, and maple permanently perfumes the air. The kiln bakes away silently in the corner. There are neatly stacked piles of tongue-and-groove paneling and neatly organized bins of trim. I'm most intrigued by little piles of oddball woods, many with big knots that some people consider junk but I consider character filled.

When I tell him there's a chance we'll paint some of the paneling, he directs me to a pile of poplar in the "oddball area." He doesn't sell enough of it, so he's trying to get rid of what's left. We only need enough for the tall wall. It'll paint up nice, it's knot-free, and he has just the quantity we need. We load it up. We install it, stand back, and realize its natural color is nearly identical to the color we were going to paint it. We slap on a coat of clear water-based polyurethane and leave it in the nude. We cover the ceilings in tongue-and-groove pine and finish it with ambered polyurethane to give it that old shellac cabin look.

We've plotted and tweaked the position of the cabin, windows, and doors to breathe in as much of Lake Superior as possible. So when it comes time to build the loft railing, we're chary. The entire time we've worked on the cabin, a lone 2×2 tacked between a few uprights has served as the railing. The view — as well as any potential fall — has been unimpeded. We want a minimalist railing, but a 2×2 lacks certain safety and aesthetic measures.

The railing will be 2 feet away from the side of the bed. Whatever it's made of, it will be the first thing we see in the morning and the last thing we see at night. Building codes dictate a railing should have no spaces large enough for a 4-inch ball to fit through. This is based on the size of a toddler's noggin. Codes also dictate a minimum height of 36 inches, a height where most people feel safe standing next to a railing without fear of ass-over-teakettling over the side. And a railing must be able to withstand 200 pounds of sideways force; no one knows where that number came from. What if you weigh 201? Since there are no building inspections for our cabin, we don't have to follow the codes, but they offer a target.

We contemplate our options. A solid wall? Zero chance. A railing with vertical pickets spaced every few inches is easy to build and common fare but can feel like a jail cell or playpen. Horizontal cable railings are unobtrusive but industrial looking. Turned spindles would be out of character. So in the end we decide on nothing — we use glass. I install 4×4 posts every 4 feet, then have a glass company cut laminated glass, the stuff used to make car windshields, to fit. I picture-frame each glass panel with three bands of trim to give a heavier feel. Picture perfect. As

Glass panels were the perfect solution to the loft railing dilemma — they blocked the sound but not the view.

a bonus the glass panels help buffer the noise between the loft and the lower level.

When it comes to the deck railing outside, we maintain the minimalist approach — both in looks and cost. We buy 3-foot lengths of threaded iron pipe, drill holes through the sides every 6 inches, secure them to the deck with $1.29 pipe flanges, stick a wood rail on top, then run braided cable through the holes to create a can-hardly-tell-it's-there railing.

No cabin is complete without a woodburning stove or fireplace, even if that cabin is in Death Valley. Gas won't suffice; you need wood so you have something to chop, carry, split, carry, stack, carry, light, poke at, stare at. You need a damper to fiddle with and ashes to clean out. Gloves dried by the fire feel warmer, bread risen by the fire tastes better, tea made from water heated in a kettle over the fire makes you cozier.

Firewood is not a problem. The thirty or forty birch trees we had to take out for the driveway and cabin lay in a pick-up-sticks pile off to the side. Birch is a curious wood. The bark can be used for everything from baskets to roofing to canoes to hats, but the same water-resistant qualities that make it so useful also contribute to its early demise. Within a year or two of being downed, it starts rotting from the inside out; it can't breathe and quickly becomes "punky." Once it's cut and split, it's fine, but you only have a few years to get on it. We need to get on it.

Dick and Jean tow their homemade log splitter over. Nothing Dick makes is wimpy; it's a gas-powered hydraulic monster that resembles a pile driver. It could split the Rock of Gibraltar. We take pause when Jean asks Dick, "Isn't that the splitter Benson was using when he lost three fingers?" But it is ten times faster and one-tenth as exhausting as swinging a maul. It wedges its way through even the crotchetiest wood. At the end of the afternoon we stand back and admire two years' worth of split wood. We feel rich. Let the power go out, let the price of propane quadruple, we've got heat.

We select a small, blue, Scandinavian-made Jøtul stove. It's built like a Rolex — functional to its core, but a little work of art all the same. The arches in the door mimic the arches in the two Gothic-arch windows in the gable ends. There are no computer chips or wires; only two small levers, one to control air intake, one to control the damper.

It's small, about the size of a car tire, but weighs 265 pounds. When they use a forklift to load it into my truck at the store, the leaf springs crouch on their haunches. At the cabin we slide it out of the truck bed onto a pair of 2×10s, then onto our Walmart dolly. The axle breaks halfway down the hill, so we wiggle, nudge, and grunt it down the hill, through the door, and onto the quarter-round hearth in the corner. Whether your cabin is 8,000 square feet with a fieldstone fireplace or 800 square feet with a dinky hearth, fire becomes the epicenter of the room.

Tom and Nan, our neighbors from the big city, come up for the weekend. We spend a few hours installing the black pipe connecting the stove to the stainless steel pipe poking through the roof. We build a small fire and stand back to watch her glow. She doesn't glow, she smokes. A lot. After a minute I remember the fiberglass insulation I'd stuffed up the stainless steel chimney to keep bugs out during construction. We don gloves, disassemble the stovepipe, pluck out the offending fiberglass, reassemble things, air out the cabin, then settle in for the first burn. It's everything we want — small, functional, delightful to the eye — smiley faces reflected in the glass door.

Kat looks up from a ragtag assortment of papers scattered across the kitchen counter. "Aah, so where did you come up with those estimates for what you thought the cabin was going to cost? From that tree house you built when you were eight?" One of the reasons we'd been able to rationalize paying an absurdly high amount for the land was that I had assured Kat that by doing the work ourselves and shopping smart we could build the cabin for an absurdly low amount.

I look over her shoulder at the tally, and it's confirmed: My cost-estimating skills are on a par with my pasta noodle estimating skills. I'm wildly off. It seemed about right. But what are you going to do now? Space the shingles twice as far apart? Thin the paint? Leave off every other deck board? Nope. Suck it up and git 'er done.

We look at reclaimed Douglas fir flooring and are floored by the price. At five dollars per square foot, the math isn't sitting right with our withering checkbook. We look at the Douglas fir flooring at a local home center, figure it's one-fourth the price and go Scroogey. It's a mistake. Douglas fir flooring from old, slow-growth trees has tight growth rings and is hard as oak. The new stuff, milled from fast-growing plantation trees, is spineless. Anything — a dragged stool, a dropped loaf of bread — leaves dents.

The floor may need to be replaced at some point, but my memories of installing it are irreplaceable. For starters, before we can lay it we need to clear everything out. It's been a hodgepodge of ladders, work lights, Frito bags, and rolls of insulation. We've never had a true sense of how the interior space would look because of the clutter. Clearing out forces us to toss, burn, and organize. At the end of the day we stand back and again see what no blueprint or architect can reveal: how a space that once existed only on paper looks in the flesh.

Kellie and I lay the floor one Saturday afternoon. She can be quiet, but when she busts loose her laugh can melt limestone. Of all the kids, she has the strongest carpentry skills. She has a great sense of design, works hard, and gets how things go together. She has "youngest child" traits — creativity, humor, idealism. She too has had to weather the uproot, the transplant, and all the compost that's gone along with it — at the age of twelve, nonetheless, when it's hard to even figure out what you're trying to figure out. It took her a while to write "Dad" instead of "Spike" on my birthday card. Sometimes I ponder how it's possible to love five kids with "all your heart" all at the same time, but that's what's happened. The math doesn't add up. Pure science will never be able to figure that one out; that's why families are magic.

We establish a routine: I cut the boards to length on the miter saw, we tap and prod the tongue-and-groove boards to fit snug, then Kellie blind-nails them to the plywood subfloor with a power nailer. She revels in the power of power nailing. It's fast, clean, noisy, and macho.

Progress is fast. The cabin is so small that 16-footers span the entire distance, meaning few seams or splices. We cut out the loose knots but leave the tighter ones because they look cool. We get the floor laid in a day.

I rent a floor sander — a bucking bronco of a thing — from Julie's Hardware. I sand the floor starting with the coarsest belts, then work my way through medium and fine grits, each grit leaving progressively smaller scratches until, to the naked eye, the floor is flat, smooth, and ready for finish. We roll on a couple of coats of water-based poly.

Building the kitchen cabinets is my initiation into the secret brotherhood of cabinetmaking. It's a task that requires not only a different set of tools from carpentry, but also a different mind-set. Everything is exposed inside and out, so the goal is to use glue and joinery, rather than screws or nails, to do most of the work. Unlike 2×4 walls that just stand there, cabinets have doors and drawers that move, bang, and swing. Not only do the components move, but the wood itself moves.

Accommodating this wood movement is one of the great puzzles woodworkers face. Though wood is clinically dead, it keeps moving. It swells in the humid summer and shrinks in the dry winter, especially across the grain. Large panels will warp if left unconfined, but crack if too rigorously contained. The challenge is clear: how does one create large doors, panels, and cabinets while controlling this irrepressible material?

Medieval cabinetmakers figured it out. They developed a system of "frame and panel" construction for creating crack-free cabinets, doors, chests, wainscot paneling, even caskets. The approach involved constructing a wood frame with grooves along the inner edges in which a large panel can float. Left free to float — unhindered by glue or nails — the panel can shrink and expand to its heart's content. Yet at the same time the frame keeps the panel from warping. Walk through any museum or antique store, and you'll find most of the surviving furniture is made of frame and panel construction. The few pieces of old solid-wood furniture you will find will be either very, very small or very, very cracked.

So when it comes time to build the cabinets it's time to put this ancient art to work. Since the floor and beams are Douglas fir, it seems fitting the kitchen cabinets should be the same. I find the perfect material by way of a two-line ad in the Building Material section: "Straight grain Doug fir, 16 ft. long, 300 boards." The salvager is an industrial arts teacher at a local high school who'd passed by the gym and heard the whining of saws and splintering of wood. He peeked his head in to find sledgehammers and circular saws annihilating the bleachers. He knew wasted wood, wasted energy, and a wasted chance when he saw them. He gained a twenty-four-hour reprieve, then, bolt by bolt, disassembled the bleachers. To the unpracticed eye these are simply old boards with three generations of bubblegum smooshed to the bottom. They're painted, and the edges are rounded over from forty years of pep rallies. Thunk one and you can hear, "Lean to the left, lean to the right . . ."

I can read Kat's eyes when I pull up with my bounty. "These don't look like kitchen cabinets to me." But under the blades of a benchtop planer the beauty is revealed. Planks that once held the adrenaline of pounding feet will soon hold our spices and Fiestaware.

I use the well-appointed workshop at the magazine — as well as the well-appointed wisdom of the editors of a woodworking magazine that share the space — to build the cabinets, doors, and drawers. I install them, then top them off with a maple butcher block top — a surface that's a countertop when you're cooking and a dining room table when you're eating.

The remaining bleacher planks I use to create the built-in window seat and surrounding shelves. The bleacher bolt holes add a nice rustic touch. It's library, guest room, and dining spot rolled into one. We've designed the seat to be long enough and wide enough for one person to sleep on, or for two people to sit face to face when eating or playing cribbage. It nestles in a little bump-out, with a 4-by-5-foot picture window overlooking the lake. We build a coffee-cup ledge into the windowsill and have cushions made from material with dragonflies on it.

The seat becomes the magnetic north of the cabin. There is no better place in the universe for reading or thinking. One friend declares it her "favorite place in the world." I sit on it now as I write these words. If I could choose one place on earth to watch a storm, read, write, ponder life, have a conversation, play gin, do nothing, play the guitar, discuss the future with one of our kids, take a nap, fool around, watch birds, do yoga, it would be this window seat. And I've done 'em all.

We buy carpet over the Internet and hire a friend of a friend of a friend to lay it. He gets started, then — maybe he's related to the plumber — disappears. He doesn't answer his phone. He doesn't return messages. We try another number and get ahold of his ex — a woman with some built-up venom. Finally we track him down — he's in jail. But his sentence is short, and he finally gets the carpet laid.

Kat begins chomping at the bit to move stuff in. I resist. Prematurely move in bar stools, and they become sawhorses. Move in a rug, and it becomes a fine place to lay a cabinet while you're belt-sanding it. Move a bed in, and those last three pieces of baseboard never, ever, ever, get installed. When it's ninety percent done, it's done — but we're at about eighty-seven.

As the cabin nears completion, I attend the National Kitchen and Bath Show in Chicago to cover new products for the magazine. It's an orgy of people, products, and flesh pressing. You can get your picture taken with the Maytag repairman, watch the Kohler shower girls twist knobs, and test drive a self-cleaning toilet with a built-in ventilation fan. Kitchen designers kick new appliance tires, and homebuilders look for new trends. There are little companies, like Vermont Soapstone, where the guy at the booth looks tortured in a suit. And there are multi-billion-dollar companies like Masco, where those manning the booth look tortured after being asked the same questions forty times.

All the basic requirements of a kitchen — refrigeration, running water, storage, appliances for cooking — were established long ago. So kitchen products have become more and more esoteric. There are lizard-shaped drawer pulls, refrigerators with built-in computers, countertops made of lava, molds for making square hard-boiled eggs. I keep an eye out for cool stuff for Oma Tupa, but we pass on the bathtub carved from solid marble and the $48,000 Grand Palais 180 stove.

I take satisfaction in a job well done, but the true moments of savoring an accomplishment are fleeting. I work two days installing landscape timbers to create stairs from the driveway down to the cabin. Cutting each 90-pound, 5-by-6-inch timber involves marking, cutting through all four sides with a circular saw, then completing the cut with a handsaw. Each step must be level, which involves hollowing out a spot with a pickax in some places and building up and compacting the earth in others. The steps, each made from five timbers, are nailed together with 10-inch spikes; this involves drilling holes, then pounding the suckers home with a 4-pound hand sledge. I treat the cut ends of the timbers with preservative to slow the inevitable rotting process. The steps need to curve so they end up square to both the deck and driveway, so I make repeated calculations and stick drawings to make sure the top step will end up at the right height and angle. I stack 100-pound boulders along the sides to hold the earth in place. It takes two hours per step and there are eleven steps.

I see progress along the way, but it isn't until the stairs are finished, swept off, the surrounding area cleaned up, and I'm sitting on the deck that I savor the completed project. That keen sense of pride lasts for the

Katie, patrolling the timber stairs

duration of one of my monthly cigarettes. The sweat on my brow and the ache in my legs makes it look, feel, and smell better than it ever will again.

Dick and Jean stop by. Since Jean's always complaining about having to slide and shuffle down the hill when visiting the cabin, I proudly announce: "I'm christening these the Jean Thorngren Memorial Steps." Dick smiles at me and says, "'Honorary' would be better. She's still got some juice left in her."

XV

TROUBLES
IN
Paradise

Mistakes are the dues you pay for living a full life.

— *Sophia Loren*

W E REVEL IN OUR NEARLY COMPLETED HAVEN. On the "How Did You Like Building Your Cabin?" questionnaire we check the "Exceeded expectations" box. But all is not — nor does it stay — perfect. The elements, utility companies, wildlife, and bonehead moves all conspire to remind us the cabin is situated in the real world.

We enter the cabin after a three-week hiatus and sense something is wrong — the sound of sloshing water and the ninety-five percent humidity provide the first clues. As we lift the trapdoor to the crawl space, our eyes behold a surreal sight: the plastic case for Kat's palm sander is floating lazily below us. As are tubes of caulk, gallons of paint, packets of sandpaper, and foam pipe insulation. As our eyes adjust we see a circular saw, drill, ten-pound box of grass seed, Sorrel boots, wood window grills, nail guns, fans, and dozens of other items submerged. The power has gone out, rendering the sump pump useless. We spend a glorious spring weekend — one we'd set aside for playing — ingloriously hauling waterlogged items out of the crawl space, setting them in the sun to dry, then hauling the fatally wounded off to the local landfill. Note to self: Buy sump pump with battery backup.

We've rearranged a lot of dirt since we bought the place. Mother Nature has had her say, too. Wind-blown sheets of ice off the lake — ice chunks that, according to Dick, have piled up as high as a three-story building — have already clawed away at the land during winter gales. This is erosion no human invention can amend or thwart.

There's also the cumulative impact of billions of raindrops, hailstones, and snowflakes hitting the earth, forming rivulets, and eating away the land, granule by granule. This is a type of erosion you can at least try to deal with. You deal with it by getting living, growing plants to grab hold of the soil. The upper leaves or blades soften the impact of the rain and hail, and the roots help knit the soil into a more stable mass.

Severe erosion on steep hills is not easy to contend with. You can't lay sod on a 60-degree incline. Grass seed doesn't stay put. Even weeds have trouble taking root because eroding land is self-cleaning; it keeps sloughing off layers of soil like eggs off Teflon.

So we decide to hydroseed the land; a process that involves mixing seed, fertilizer, straw, fish emulsion, water, green dye, and some secret ingredients together in a huge tank, then spraying the mixture in a blanket across the terrain. Definitely not a DIY project. Capillary action delivers water to the seeds and keeps them moist. The process gives each little grass seed a little fertilizer to gnaw on, water to nourish it, and straw to limit evaporation and help "knit" it onto the surface. The secret ingredients help the mixture stick to the land. It's like creating the world's largest Chia Pet. A two-thousand-dollar Chia Pet.

Selecting the hydroseeder is easy; there's only one in the area, and they're sixty miles south in Duluth. The most cost-effective approach is to bring in an entire tankful of the mix and spread it until it's gone. We're looking for the toughest damn ground cover we can find, so we decide on a mixture nicknamed MN DOT 500 — the mix road crews use to stabilize the soil after road construction. It needs no maintenance, grows fast, and is tough. The one big unknown is the weather. Hydroseed can withstand a light rain, but get a gully washer and you wind up with two thousand dollars' worth of seed on the shore of Lake Superior. We're watching the sky and rubbing the rabbit's foot.

Three workers with a trailer and blending tank the size of a small moving van arrive. Step A is to broadcast twenty-five pounds of grass seed across the bare soil to supplement the seed in the tank. Step B is to unreel 200 feet of firefighting-size hose and drag the end as far downhill as possible. Step C is to turn the pump on and scramble like hell. The worker manning the nozzle is part fireman, part alligator wrestler, and part spray-paint artist. He sprays the cliffs, the hills, and a few upturned tree stumps for good measure. The land looks like it's been papier-mâchéd.

We all help drag the hose uphill as work progresses. When the hose stops spraying, the nozzle man shouts "kink," and everyone scrambles to find the bend. There's enough hydroseed to cover the big cliff, swatches along both sides of the cabin, and another hill along the driveway. We pray for sprinkles − light sprinkles − and wait for the seed to germinate. Mother Nature is kind, providing cool weather and many light rains. The hydroseed grows into a lush, thick meadow. It's a lawn that will never be mowed, never feel the click of a croquet ball, never be the envy of any neighbors − except those who have erosion problems. This is grass with a job to do. This is blue-collar bluegrass.

⸻

All is good. But we wake one morning after arriving late, look out the loft window, and realize something is missing. Part of the hill. A massive clump of five birch trees perched near the top has busted loose and snowplowed tons of dirt − hydroseeded land and all − down to the shoreline. The trees come to rest on the beach. To add insult the clump winds up in a position so it looks like a gigantic hand flipping us the bird. Our hard-fought battle with erosion is lost.

We get Bradley to come in and yank out any other trees perched along the edge of the hill that might perform similar feats of destruction. We bring in truckloads of riprap — sharp-edged, dynamited rock that can bite into a hill — to stabilize the earth. We reseed the hill, this time by hand, and put down 6-by-50-foot rolls of erosion mat. This summer being at the cabin is the antithesis of what being at the cabin should be about. We have erosion on the brain. We plot ways to stop it. We agonize over the havoc we've wreaked on the land. Everything had been fine for 10,000 years, and then we showed up. It's only when the hill has been stabilized for a few years, but our bank account eroded, that we can relax again.

A few years later Mother Nature kicks us in the arse again. I've built steps down to the lake. It requires building five landings out of landscape timbers, and five sets of zigzagging staircases. Eighty steps in all. Everything is hauled by hand — my hand. I arrive on opening day of spring and head down the stairs to see how the canoe and kayak have fared over the winter. Halfway down I see the bottom half of the stairway in shambles — busted stair jacks, treads flung everywhere, landings demolished. WTF? First I imagine strong winds have blown ice floes into the stairs, smashing them like a hydraulic car crusher. But the lowest section is undamaged. It can't be hail or wind. Maybe it's been hit by an engine cowl from a jet. It happens. No cowl. Vandals? Nah. The only thing I can figure out is that a bear or moose, either chasing or being chased, has scrambled up the steps, demolishing them in the process.

I cringe as I walk up the surviving stairs to the cabin; another week of work has appeared out of nowhere. As I reach the top of the stairs I again notice something missing: a ten-ton boulder that had once sat behind — but now I'm thinking had been held in place by — a small birch. It's not missing, it's relocated. I follow its trajectory along one set of stairs, through another set, into the landing, past the kayak — and there it is, snickering down on the shoreline. Mostly what I think is, "Damn, that woulda been cool to see."

Winter also decides to pitch in. One frigid January day, Kat heads north with four "Women on the Edge," her dogsledding and sailing friends. No one has been to the cabin in a month. As they near Oma Tupa in complete darkness, Kat prepares her weekend mates for the worst-case scenario. Three things could put a wee bit of a damper on their weekend. One, there's a chance Bradley hasn't plowed the driveway, which means they'll need to carry all their stuff — including a sheik's ransom in wine — down the hill. No problem. Two, the wind may have blown out the wall

A rolling stone may gather no moss, but it wreaked havoc on the stairs leading to the lake. The kayak survived a near-death experience.

furnace pilot light and there would be no heat; a situation easily remedied by firing up the woodstove. No problem. Three, the pipes could be frozen and five women could be without water or plumbing for the weekend. Problem.

They arrive to find the driveway 2 feet deep in snow. After trudging down the hill, they find the cabin a Siberian 25 degrees. The pipes are frozen. They get a fire cranking to warm the place up, and lo and behold, they hear the sweet flow of water — flowing through a busted pipe under the kitchen sink.

They find a plumber who miraculously agrees to come out on a Friday evening. There is a God. The plumber has to trudge all his equipment, tools, and pipe down the pitch-black hill. He phones me from underneath the crawl space to ask a question about how the pipes are routed. I hear the stomping of five very possibly inebriated women dancing to Donna Summer's "Hot Stuff" on the floor above. He needs one little part to finish the job, so he trudges back up the hill, drives back to his shop, then hits a deer with his van on the way back. He borrows a car from a guy near the scene of the accident and returns to finish the job. By the time he gets back and calls me with one final question, Kat and company are lip-synching into hairbrushes to the soundtrack of *Dirty Dancing*.

I can't wait for *this* bill to come: overtime on a Friday night, totaled van, four trips by foot up and down our avalanche of a driveway, combat pay for working in the dwarf-height crawl space. And for good measure, throw in a sexual harassment lawsuit for all the pipe jokes they've shouted down to him. Might as well just hand over the keys to the place and call it even.

But crazy-dancing to Bon Jovi with four friends until two in the morning on a cold winter night with heat and water? Priceless.

The northern winds and power company also conspire to make us miserable. When the power goes out, the wall furnace fan — thus the wall furnace — won't work. If strong winds blow out the pilot light — a common occurrence — same thing.

After the third case of furnace malfunction and broken pipes we install a freeze alarm. We find one that automatically calls three phone numbers, every hour, when the cabin temperature drops below 45 degrees. After reading the instruction manual equivalent of *War and Peace*, I figure out how to program the thing. We head home, with renewed peace of mind — until an hour down the road my cell phone rings, and I note on caller ID someone is calling us from the cabin. Strange. "There is an alert at your monitored location." We know there's not an alert — we've just been there and the cabin was 70 degrees. But the alarm — gone anthropomorphic like the Plymouth Fury in Stephen King's *Christine* — continues to call and call and call. We arrive home to find six long-distance messages from the alarm on our landline.

I've forgotten the code number that will allow us to turn the damn thing off at the cabin. Like a monkey trying to type the Constitution, I start punching in possible code numbers, I finally figure out the code — but only after "Christine" has placed fourteen long-distance calls.

And then there are things that bug you. In most states people plan outdoor events based on the weather; in Minnesota, events are planned according to insects.

"We were considering a backyard August wedding, until we realized Sherry couldn't fit the mosquito netting over her veil."

"We moved Harold's bar mitzvah to May so we wouldn't have to fish so many box elder bugs out of the punch bowl." And so on.

We had encountered our share of bugs while building — a hornet nest in the rafters here, a squadron of mosquitoes there — but the bug world isn't able to truly organize itself into pestilent squadrons until the cabin is finished. They come in three waves.

Wave #1: Tent caterpillars. The small white moths that crash insanely into your outdoor lights and windows at night don't start life as incredibly annoying moths, they start life as incredibly annoying caterpillars. In Wallenda-like moves they lower themselves via mucous strings onto your head, into your salad, or, if you're about to capture the specter of a bald eagle rising out of the lake with a trout in its talons, on your camera lens. They feast on birch and poplar leaves with such abandon that they can – and do – denude entire forests. They don't smell that great when you step on them. And the crowning glory of these creatures of God comes when they finally disappear. They disappear by weaving sticky cotton ball masses positioned in places that, according to the International Tent Moth Building Code, must be "slightly beyond the reach of a standard broom" and be positioned so as to add "maximum ugliness to a structure." Even on a dwelling as small as Oma Tupa, they number in the thousands.

Wave #2: Asian beetles. For starters they look like ladybugs in drag with bad makeup. The cuteness of the nursery rhyme "Ladybug, ladybug, fly away home; your house is on fire and your children will burn" becomes a passionate desire to set fire to the things after you've used the Dust Buster to suck up the four thousandth one. When vacuumed they emit a "yellow, foul-smelling substance" as a defense. Their favorite prank is sneaking into unattended cans of Coke. And when cornered, the little thugs bite.

Wave #3: Cluster flies. As fall approaches they seek a warm place to hibernate and are drawn to the crevices around the windows of the cabin. Somehow they squeeze through the labyrinth of siding, trim, Tyvek, caulk, plywood, insulation, drywall, and interior trim. To celebrate their arrival they break dance on their backs until they die. Upon entering the cabin after a long absence, it is not unusual to find hordes of them. They are a midlevel annoyance; irritating on the same level as cotton balls stuffed into the necks of aspirin bottles and your niece who puts tomato knives pointy end up in the dishwasher rack.

Bugs aren't the only squatters in this tenement. We enter one day and notice the afghan that was left flung over the back of the couch has started mysteriously unraveling. We're awakened that night by the obsessive-compulsive crumpling of insulation paper backing within the walls. Then we discover a bag of marshmallows is missing. Finally, we encounter the artifact that would instill fear into the heart of even Genghis Khan — the dreaded mouse turd. On further investigation we discover this rodent has consumed unfathomable quantities of food. This is a mouse with an eating disorder of great magnitude: a bag of gorp, a pack of saltines, a pound of elbow macaroni, my beloved Krusteaz waffle mix – all ransacked with only a cache of the rice-size turds left as a thank-you.

Kat spends the weekend Tupperware-izing every morsel in sight. We break out the expanding foam and fill gaps and crevices; lay out d-CON, mousetraps and any other weapons of mass mouse destruction we can find at Julie's Hardware. We win the battle and, thus far, the war.

Even the virtuous trees screw with us. Six large dead birches start aiming kamikaze branch attacks toward the cabin during high winds. It's them or us. I break out the chain saw and warm up by taking out the harmless ones — ones that could fall in any direction without endangering person, place, or thing.

I cut a notch in the trunk on the side I want the tree to fall, then cut downward at an angle from the opposite side so the tree is hinged and "swings" in the direction of the notch. I'm a respectable seventy-five percent accurate with my practice trees, so I go after the one closest to the cabin. It's leaning away from the cabin, but even so I tell Kat to watch from the corner of the deck, so she's out of harm's way.

I notch the tree so it will fall away from the cabin, then make the angled back cut. I react with the swiftness of an arthritic clam as the tree falls — without hesitation — directly toward the cabin. Instinctively I give the plummeting trunk one gigantic shoulder block — enough to direct it away from the cabin directly toward the deck and Kat. Kat vaults to safety, but the furniture isn't as quick. The tree hits a kidney-shaped teak table as if laser guided. Seeing the cartoon way the table expires is almost worth the two hundred bucks we're out as the tree hits and eighty table parts explode upward in a Wile E. Coyote shower of kindling. Not one surviving glue joint. No semblance of tableness whatsoever. Clearly at least a second-place finish on *America's Funniest Home Videos*.

But there's more arboreal mischief. My sister Patty and husband Ray head to the cabin for a much-needed weekend away. Two hours after their projected arrival, I get a phone call.

"Aaah — we're stuck in the driveway."

This is technically impossible; it's June, they have an SUV, and they're headed downhill.

"Aaah — when we left a few days ago it was fine," I blather, not so much sarcastically as accusingly.

"Yah, but I bet when you left a few days ago there wasn't a big friggin' tree lying across the driveway."

They'd gotten halfway down the driveway, belatedly spotted a massive pine the wind had toppled, then spun their wheels, hopelessly trying to back up the hill in the loose gravel. They could go neither to nor fro.

"You got a chain saw somewhere around here? Ray's been trying to chop through this thing with some kind of weird-looking hatchet for the last hour."

I explain to Patty they can find the chain saw in the crawl space. But curiosity has the best of me. "Could you text a photo of what's going on?"

A minute later the photo arrives. I zoom in on Ray's progress. The divot he's chopped in the trunk looks like the work of a carpenter ant with severe attention deficit disorder. I zoom in on Ray's weapon of choice and see he's selected a terminally dull five-pound splitting maul. I'm so giggle-shook I can't return the text for five minutes. The following Christmas Ray presents me with a varnished disc of wood sliced from the offending tree.

But while there's plenty of trouble in paradise, ninety percent of the time Oma Tupa is paradise.

XVI

SETTLING IN, *Grooving* OUT

There's more to life than increasing its speed.

— *attributed to Mohandas K. Gandhi*

William Morris, the nineteenth-century English craftsman, wrote, "Have nothing in your houses which you do not know to be useful or believe to be beautiful." Kat and I agree, but we cast a pretty wide net when it comes to "beautiful." An Amish bent twig rocker, a sixties spaceship floor lamp, a colored pencil sketch of a gay peacock, and funny-shaped rocks have all moseyed into the cabin.

Some purchases are more strategic. We transport a hide-a-bed sofa (our guest bedroom) in the Dakota; then, rather than wait fifteen torturous minutes for Tessa and a friend to arrive to help, the two of us wrestle it in. It's got some tonnage. We Laurel-and-Hardy it 10 feet out of the truck, leap it forward, and roll one end on a dolly. It springs open. We girdle it with a bungee cord, then push and slide. We haven't learned much since moving the woodstove. We can't get it through either door, and we're thinking we either have an outdoor hide-a-bed or need to disassemble the patio door. We finally hook-shot it in. We roll out a rug made from carpet scraps, then plunk the couch down.

The cabin is so small that we move the rug and couch fractions of an inch to get them positioned right. With the hide-a-bed extended, we can't have overnight guests burning their toes on the woodstove. Nor can we have it block the wall furnace. We spend a prolonged length of time debating the exact position of this and other things, then realize,

"We're not epoxy-gluing these things in place. We can move them, right? Move them a lot if we want."

For me, moving stuff in is just another step in the building process, but for Kat this is huge. From conception through morning sickness through labor, this is her baby. And at night when I would dream about roof angles and trim details, she would dream about paint swatches and furniture. She is now the foreman and I, the gopher.

⊶━━━━⊷

On the way to the cabin one afternoon, Kat expounds on the collateral benefits of building the cabin. Prior to building, we were neurotically wishy-washy. Part of this came from merging families late in life where everything from child-rearing philosophies to brand of toothpaste needed to be jibed, negotiated, or at least understood. And to do that we would often default to "what-do-you-think?" mode; the stakes were so high — and so human.

But building the cabin was a safe place to express full-blown opinions; a safe playground for working out differences; a litmus test for likes and dislikes. I'm inclined toward funky, Kat is more classic. I like old, Kat prefers new. I like eccentric and whimsical, Kat is more traditional. So we speak our minds, then hash out details about bar stools, bookshelves, and barbecue grills. The cabin becomes a playground for exercising some new communication muscles.

⊶━━━━⊷

Spending time at the cabin drags out old memories that have slumbered for years. The air, the relaxed feel, the pace bring me back forty years to summer weekends at The Roost. To evenings when I would listen through the heat duct to the adults laughing, drinking martinis, and playing bridge in the next room. To long, rainy afternoons when I was allowed to drink sinful amounts of Coke and do nothing but read comic books. To days when the best toys came off wheel rims — inner tubes for floating, tire swings dangling from dangerously frayed ropes, half-inflated tractor tires for trampolines. It transports me back to afternoons when I would help my grandfather, a tight-laced lawyer turned weekend woodsman, fillet and skin sunnies. If the gods were smiling, he'd let me slip a few shells into his .22 and shoot cans perched on a log next to the outhouse. And if it was a full house, I'd drift off to sleep on a rocking glider on the screen porch or, best of all, on a green canvas World War I army cot we'd unfold, click together, and nestle against the living room wall.

And sometimes the flashbacks transport me back twenty years to the cabin my parents bought on Lake Waverly. They bring back bitter-sweet memories of the two old theater seats my father bolted to the end of the dock for watching boats and the world go by. I'd auction off a year of my life for the chance to sit side by side with him on those seats for five minutes today. All of these dust-covered memories are blown bare as the Superior winds blow hard.

Since the days we started looking for land, I've kept random notes about our cabin venture in a ragtag selection of notebooks, laptop folders, and napkin backs. Bringing order to these scraps of thought is something I've longed to do. Maybe there's a book there.

Kat is 110 percent behind the idea of my taking a short leave of absence to do this. When she left her job to start PrimeStaff, I kept the ship afloat. The risk paid off. So there's a certain rightness to it.

I head north to write. Twenty miles up the road my cell phone rings and I hear sobs. Not little sniffling sobs, but deep guttural, whole-hearted sobs. Kat sobs. I pull over. Trying to decipher a few words, I think one of the kids has been in an accident.

"No, no."

Then my imagination switches to Kat's friend, Beven, who's been battling cancer for years. "Did Beven die? Is that it?"

"No, no."

Finally she calms down. Her mammogram has come back with suspicious spots. The doctor would like her to come back the next day for more tests. There's an urgency about it.

Kat tells me to keep aiming north; my returning home won't solve anything. Okay. I drive 100 feet north and do a Steve McQueen U-turn. We talk, hug, and hold for an hour, then I head north again in earnest. The long drive provides plenty of time to swing deals. "Lord, if things turn out all right I'll change my wicked ways." "Kat, if you pull out of this okay, I'll never take you or your breasts for granted again."

And when I'm at the cabin that night I realize without Kat, without someone to share the space, tranquility, bliss, and views with, the cabin is just four bored walls perched above a lonely lake. Tom Waits growls:

> What makes a house grand,
> Ain't the roof or the doors.
> If there's love in a house,
> It's a palace for sure.
> Without love, it ain't nothin' but a house —
> A house where nobody lives.

Same is true of a cabin.

The next day the phone rings, and it's Kat, reporting in with joy. The second round of tests shows the spots are pinched pieces of skin or flaws in the X-ray or something, but not cancer.

Okay, Spike, remember, you made some deals here.

In her vastly entertaining book, *Shelter* — a book that is ostensibly about building a cabin but, in reality, is thirty-two percent about bad dates, forty-one percent about childhood memories, twenty-two percent about the land the cabin is built on, and five percent about actually building the place — Sarah Stonich talks about a man she meets and marries during the project. His hearing is subpar; thus they make a ritual of twice a day sitting on the fish house bed, face to face, the rest of the world shut out, discussing matters great and small. It keeps them connected. Which is the purpose of every cabin: to make the world smaller, to slow you down and allow you to focus on the important people and events — even if your hearing is perfect and you don't have a fish house bed.

We all need a cabin — whether it has four walls or not. We all need a destination, an activity, or a group of people to tow us through the midweek muck. A cabin can be a motorcycle, a golf course, a table at Starbucks where you gather with friends. It's worth asking the question: Do we work five days a week and jam our Saturdays with chores, all so we can do the things we really enjoy — lead the lives we want to lead — for a few hours on Sunday? Maybe we need to change the ratio.

There's this story.

A Mexican fisherman meets a New York City businessman vacationing near his village. The banker asks the fisherman what he does all day.

"I get up at ten, fish for a few hours, eat lunch, take a siesta, make love to my wife, have a beer, then spend the evening with friends."

The banker lectures, "Why do that? You should get up at seven, fish for five hours, take a thirty-minute lunch break, then fish for another five hours."

"Why?" asks the fisherman.

"That way you can earn a lot of money, buy another boat, and expand your business."

"Why would I do that?" asks the fisherman.

"So you can earn even more money, hire more people, maybe open your own fish market."

"Why would I do that?" responds the fisherman.

"So in thirty years you can retire. That way you can get up at ten, fish for a few hours, take a siesta, make love to your wife, and spend time with friends."

The cabin is used a lot — by us, by the kids, by friends seeking refuge. In the early stages it's easy to offhandedly offer "cabin rights" to helpers and friends. "Hey, we want it used, if you ever need a place to . . ." And now that it's done, people take us up on that. We don't know where to draw the line. A kid? No problem. A sister and spouse? Fine. A Top Ten friend of Kat or mine? Sure. A friend of a friend? Well, uh, okay. A second cousin of a step-uncle? Ah, well, we'll see if anyone will be up there that weekend.

Things happen. Ken, a friend and coworker, is heading north to camp with his son Frankie and needs a place to lay over for a night. They arrive late, and Ken thinks it would be a good idea for Frankie to sled down an unknown, uncharted driveway in pitch blackness on the sled we keep on top of the driveway for hauling material. Frankie zips down the driveway, hits a snow-covered mound of dirt, and catapults like "the agony of defeat" ski jumper onto a ledge 30 feet down the hill. There are no lights, no ropes, and oooh, it's below zero. Ken ties extension cords together and rappels down the cliff to rescue his offspring.

But most visits are calmer. We buy a little blank book for visitors to write in, and it slowly fills with memories, thank-yous, and thoughts about life. The place brings out the closet poet. One musician friend writes, "As the leaves, like silent wall flowers at a junior high dance, were stirred to join in the night music, the evening felt electric yet filled with peace." In a less romantic vein another friend writes, "Warning to future Carlsen guests — no matter how they beg, whine, and wheedle DO NOT agree to play SCRABBLE with these people. They will beat your pants off!"

From the book one can ascertain that the two main activities are (1) sitting on the point doing nothing and (2) sitting in the window seat doing nothing. It just depends on the weather. A landscaper friend who stays there sketches a plan for a fire pit, along with a note that suggests we buy "Charlie Brown trees" — nursery rejects — to plant along the edge because they'll look natural. Someday we'll build it.

Two impromptu honeymoons transpire. Various friends celebrate fiftieth, thirty-fourth, and tenth anniversaries there. Our kids use it for reunions, marathon headquarters, minivacations, and solitary retreats. We're happy to share our little slice of heaven, despite the fact everyone puts the cheese grater back in a different drawer.

My mother and her ninety-three-year-old husband, Frank, accompany us for a weekend. They're a little brittle afoot, so we stay put and play Scrabble, Yahtzee, cribbage, and bridge. Frank, so competitive he goes for the throat when playing "Go to the Dump" with his grandkids, is in his glory. It's endearing to hear them giggle like high school kids on the foldout couch down below at night. We overhear Frank whispering, "I haven't lost a game all weekend."

By the time we get Oma Tupa finished we have four kids in college, and Kat and I find ourselves living on a semester basis. We too get tests, but of a psychological nature as the kids filter in with their academic triumphs, fears, piercings, boyfriends, girlfriends, and surprises.

We all rendezvous at the cabin before Christmas to reconnect. The first night we stay up until 2:30 a.m. chatting and playing games. The next day is spent cooking soup, splitting wood, playing gin, talking, and napping. Zach, the lone boy amidst a sea of four sisters and a deep thinker, is inclined to pull into his shell, but even he goes with the flow. Kat plays a game or two of solitaire — an event that marks her unwinding. A fire burns in the Jøtul. Alison Krauss is singing. Day fades into night.

And I think in my own fantastical way of thinking that this is one of the few times in life when I know everyone in our family is safe. There is no danger. I can see, touch, and protect everyone. There are no cars, boyfriends, girlfriends, poisons, or terrorists flying planes into buildings. We have a forest-worth of firewood to keep us warm, an endless supply of fresh water, sleeping spots for everyone. No plagues can reach us. We could all grow old here. I want to quarantine everyone. I enjoy this ultimate sense of security for the few hours I can.

The round-top window in the loft stretches from ceiling to floor, making it the perfect perch for sitting crisscross applesauce to watch the sky lay a hand on the lake. At night, when the lake is in irons and reflecting glassy smooth, you get twice as much star, moon, and calm for the money. When the sky is frenzied, and the lake angry, and lightning 300 miles away searches you out, you're glad to have a seat in the covered section of the world. From that window, the curvature of the world sets the horizon thirteen miles out — and to watch the phantom smokestack of a freighter sixteen miles out moonwalk across the lake confirms the world is a magic place. God left a little part of it all unknown for the artist in us to enjoy.

We buy a house in the historic town of Stillwater, a house built in 1850, which, to the best of our research, is the oldest house standing. We can walk three blocks to Len's corner store, a coffee shop, and Nelson's Ice Cream parlor, home of the ice cream cone the size of cauliflower. We hear wedding bands playing by the river. Church bells clang at 6:00 p.m., and we create a tradition during the thirty seconds of chiming, we stop what we're doing, breathe deep, and count our blessings. If we can't pause for half a minute, there's a problem.

The town is ideal; the house, not so much. On the disclosure form that asks the seller to list all known problems, the widow we are buying the house from writes "Broken soap dispenser in dishwasher." In her mind the house is mint. I've inspected the house and know we're dealing with more than a twelve-dollar part. We replace the boiler, hot water heater, and roof. The foundation bows outward more than a foot, and the front porch is so rotten the roof stays in place only out of habit. The wiring is the original knob-and-tube wiring from 1895; it's still functional, but as we remodel our way through the house, we replace it.

We buy the house in order to downsize, but whoa, wouldn't a garage be nice? And while we're at it, wouldn't it make sense to put living space above it? And wouldn't it be convenient to move the laundry room up out of that musty *Nightmare on Elm Street* basement? And how about a second bathroom? And an entryway? And an extra bedroom? And a little second-story deck overlooking town? And it turns out to be a mammoth, year-long project.

We barely take a deep breath between finishing the cabin and launching into this project. Living day to day amid the sawdust, mess, and decision making is less fun than visiting it for a few days. We take out exterior walls and the house gets so cold the water in the washing machine freezes. We hope for money, old letters, or historic newspapers in the walls but only find carpenter ants — journeymen carpenter ants — and asbestos.

As the project drags on we do less work ourselves and hire others to do more. It costs more, but we save on marriage-counseling bills. I feel one-dimensional; all I do is build, think about building, write about building, dream about building. Kat likes order, and all we have is disorder. We vow to take a break for a year or two before embarking on any other building projects. We vow to take time to use the cabin.

For three years we've been so absorbed in building the cabin that our old canoe, "The Barge," has sat unpaddled by the shoreline. Finally, one perfect summer day Kat and I break out the paddles and wrestle the thing into the water. We paddle north along the shore and are surprised the point isn't really a point, but an outjutting of land large enough to accommodate four substantial cabins. We discover a sea cave, a cave I'll explore when Kat isn't along; dark caves full of water are not on her to-do list. We find mini-islands with gull colonies dotting the shoreline.

I thought of our cabin as isolated since we could only see two dwellings from where it sits, but we're just one of a strand of pearls draped around Superior's neck.

We paddle south and find sculptural rock formations and lava flows thrust skyward by earthquakes and shifting tectonic plates. We encounter more bays, thumper holes, and caves. We pass a weird column we christen "The Boot," only to discover the formation is known to the locals as The Boot. We find another rock formation in the shape of a large easy chair that we nickname "The Lazy Boy Chair." We spend the rest of a lazy morning sitting face to face on it, listening to the water from Kennedy Creek cascade into the lake.

We see no other canoeists or kayakers in the three hours we're out. Near larger cities you see more boat traffic because there are more people. In the absolute wilderness you encounter more people, because people go there in a like-minded mass escape. But we're in an area with few houses, where few people journey. We're in a fall-between-the-cracks kind of place.

From the time we strike a deal with Dick and Jean until we hammer a few coat hooks in the closet, two years slide by. In some ways it seems like we've been building Oma Tupa for decades. Yet in others it seems like it's been only weeks since we stood on the shore looking up trying to figure out how financially and physically we could climb that slippery slope.

Some will argue a cabin is a poor investment. You could take the money spent and buy a month of vacation every year at the poshest of resorts for a lifetime and still come out ahead. It's one more place to pay taxes, insurance, and utilities. It's one more dwelling to paint and another drippy faucet to fix. All of this for a place to spend thirty days a year.

But it's not just a thirty-day affair. Knowing it's there helps us get through the other three hundred and thirty-five days. Knowing it's waiting for us with open arms makes a stressful workday a little calmer. When the world seems too large and too complex, the cabin is small and simple.

AFTERWORD

Writing a book like *Cabin Lessons* is like rummaging through an old box of papers in the basement. You start out looking for a birth certificate, but as you search through old photos, letters, report cards, and silhouette cutouts, you find dog-eared things that make you grin, crinkly things that make you sad, and dusty things that stir up long-forgotten stories. Pretty soon it's two in the morning, you sit surrounded by this pile of faded memories, and you've become this kind of happy-sad Jell-O-ish thing.

Searching through a mildewed 12-by-12-inch box and writing a 6-by-8-inch book hold some common ground: Both distill life down to its essence. Both can throw an emotional punch. You're forced to take memories that are inchoate, perhaps never put into words, and give them shape. And you can never get all the old stuff to fit back into the box; a few things linger — and that's okay. We all get to write the narrative of our life whether we write it down or not. I'm grateful for the chance to have sparred with the past while writing this book.

Dick and Jean moved a few years ago. They bought a house on the fringes of Silver Bay; a place big enough for Dick to support his riding lawn mower habit but small enough so Jean didn't feel as though she were running the Ponderosa. They finally had the time and resources to pursue a few well-earned dreams. They bought a whale of an RV and traveled the country. Dick bought a boat and built a woodworking shop. A little while passed, and Dick started needing oxygen and Jean started feeling a little foggy, so they moved to an assisted living place nearby. They started coasting a little. One Tuesday Dick drove to Two Harbors and traded in their ailing SUV for a more dependable vehicle. On Wednesday he made sure the lease on their apartment was good for another year. Jean was set. He died on Thursday.

When someone cuts a larger-than-life figure, he leaves a larger-than-life hole in your life when he exits. We miss Dick's fish cakes, his Ole and Lena jokes, and the sound of his four-wheeler coming down the driveway. But mostly we miss his steadiness. I've changed careers, Kat's business has had its ups and downs, our kids have scattered, we've had to wrestle down a few demons, grandkids have arrived on the scene, Kat's mom died, but through it all, spending time with Dick every few weeks was like pulling into the calm waters of Crystal Bay during a storm. Ain't that somethin'?

Building stuff can become a sort of a touchstone for your own mortality. I remember when carrying a sheet of three-quarter-inch plywood was a study in tranquility; now I grunt just toting a half-incher. Life sneaks up on you. One day you look in the mirror and see you've got wrinkly elbows. The next day you've got a little boulevard of hair growing in your ears. You start paying attention to those reverse mortgage ads on TV; I guess that's just how it's gonna go down.

A lot of waves have belly-flopped into the thumper hole since we built Oma Tupa. The cabin hasn't changed much — that "When it's ninety percent done, it's done" maxim holds a lot of water; maybe we're at ninety-one-and-a-half percent now — but other things have changed.

The land has changed some. The thumper hole is 3/10,000ths of an inch deeper. Erosion keeps pecking away at the cliffs — an optimist might say it's less land to weed-whack, but I'd be more comfortable with a ceasefire. An ice storm hit one May when the birches were leafed out. Birches tend to be short-lived anyway, but in just a few hours half the trees took a knee and the other half became distorted in strange yet wonderful ways. Some branches were whiplashed into 360-degree loops and zigzags; some trunks were folded into right angles. On the bright side, one day I'll harvest these misfits to create a chair, and people will ask, "How the hell did he do that?"

As much as we feel secure in our cabin, we're surrounded by uncertainty. The lot to one side sold. It's zoned Resort Commercial. One day I ran across surveyors staking out a spot for what they said was going to be a B&B, but no dozers yet.

On our other side sit forty acres of state land, its future unknowable and uncontrollable.

The bike trail, which weaves and bobs between the lake and Highway 61, from Two Harbors up to Grand Marais, will pass by — or cut through — our land someday, but "someday" has yet to come. A "kayak highway" is being established along the shoreline. The state-owned land next to us is a designated camping spot, but it's rarely used; in a busy year two tents get pitched.

So for now, we sit and cherish.

Kat and I have been working with the Mission Tanzania group from our church, helping build a secondary school and establish a tree farm in Central Tanzania. After working there, we realize Oma Tupa, by any standards, isn't small, but palatial; isn't simple, but elaborate; that our water system isn't primitive, but a privilege. We complain a whole lot less about — well — everything.

The quaintness, closeness, and easy maintenance of a small cabin has served us well. But now — when we add up kids, spouses, and enough grandkids to form a small scrum — the census has doubled. A cabin's role is to promote intimacy, not privacy, but at some point intimacy can sort of sneak into chaos. You can only pile dishes so high in the sink or stack so many suitcases in the entry. A small cabin is romantic, but get too many people, and romance of any kind is difficult.

We've started doodling ways of creating more space. It could be as simple as erecting a big canvas army surplus tent on a platform. Or putting a basement under the cabin (which would put a final finality to the leaning post issue). Or maybe we'd tack a small structure to the side of the cabin. Kat keeps clipping out pictures of bunkhouse rooms from *Martha Stewart Living* magazines, and they *do* look fun. I can see how a space like that could work the cabin DNA into our kids and grandkids. Whatever we do, we'll keep the same feel — it will just be a *larger* same feel.

One day while I am at the store and Kat is out yanking weeds, an Italian-made convertible rumbles down the driveway, oil pan tempting fate. The dapper driver — also Italian made — and the blonde in the passenger seat — maybe California made — get out and stretch.

"This is the most beautiful place I've ever seen," he exalts, stretching and feeling most at home. His companion agrees.

"Yes, we love it here," Kat explains.

They walk around, then turn to Kat.

"We love it more. How much do you want for it?"

"Thank you, but it's not for sale."

"Just name your price. Everything has a price," he counters. But Kat just smiles.

Ain't that somethin'?

Oma Tupa has become part of Kat and me. We're neither tourists nor residents in our Lake Superior abode — we are cabin-ites. We don't do the thirty-mile-per-hour, neck-craning tourist thing as we poke up Highway 61, nor do we take the antsy-pants pass-everything-in-sight locals approach. We know the people at Julie's Hardware well enough to talk about the weather but not well enough to talk about our kids. We're not starstruck by the lake, nor do we take it for granted. We don't stop to pick birch branches by the side of the road, but if there's a full moon over Superior as we drive up at night, we still pull over in wonder.

Oma tupa, oma lupa.
(One's cabin, one's freedom.)

FOR FURTHER READING

Banschick, Mark R., and David Tabatsky. *The Intelligent Divorce*, rev. ed. Intelligent Book Press, 2010.

Deal, Ron L. *The Smart Stepfamily*, rev. ed. Bethany House Publishers, 2014.

Mahan, John, and Ann Mahan. *Lake Superior Story and Spirit*. Sweetwater Visions, 1998.

Marrone, Teresa. *The Seasonal Cabin Cookbook*. Adventure Publications, 2001.

Mulfinger, Dale, and Susan E. Davis. *The Cabin*. Taunton Press, 2001.

National Association of Home Builders. "Housing Facts, Figures & Trends 2004," National Association of Home Builders, 2004.

Ratigan, William. *Great Lakes Shipwrecks & Survivals*, rev. ed. Wm. B. Eerdmans Publishing Co., 1977.

Rutstrum, Calvin. *The Wilderness Cabin*, 4th ed. Macmillan, 1975.

Stiles, David and Jeanie. *Cabins*. Firefly Books, 2001.

U.S. Army Corps of Engineers. Great Lakes Water Levels fact sheet. U.S. Army Corps of Engineers.

OTHER BOOKS BY SPIKE CARLSEN

The Backyard Homestead Book of Building Projects
Discover more than 75 useful structures to make your backyard more productive, from cold frames and workbenches to chicken coops and flowerpot smokers.
296 pages. Paper. ISBN 978-1-61212-085-0.

Woodworking FAQ
Carlsen presents practical answers to common woodworking questions, plus insider tips on how to be successful in every project.
304 pages. Paper with partially concealed wire-o. ISBN 978-1-60342-729-6.

MORE STOREY BOOKS YOU WILL ENJOY

Compact Cabins by Gerald Rowan
Find simple living in 1,000 square feet or less — featuring 62 design interpretations for every taste.
216 pages. Paper. ISBN 978-1-60342-462-2.

The Good Life Lab by Wendy Jehanara Tremayne
Follow and learn from the adventures of a resourceful couple who ditched their careers and rebuilt their lives from the ground up, making their own fuel, structures, food, and medicine.
320 pages. Paper. 978-1-61212-101-7.

Keep Out! by Lee Mothes
Build and customize a clubhouse, with friendly and accessible step-by-step illustrated instructions and handy hints for kids and families looking for a fun backyard project.
224 pages. Paper. ISBN 978-1-61212-029-4.

These and other books from Storey Publishing are available wherever quality books are sold or by calling 1-800-441-5700. Visit us at *www.storey.com* or sign up for our newsletter at *www.storey.com/signup*.